Accounting for Business

Accounting for Business

Practicalities and Strategies

Roger Hussey and Audra Ong

BEP

BUSINESS EXPERT PRESS

Leader in applied, concise business books

Accounting for Business: Practicalities and Strategies

Copyright © Business Expert Press, LLC, 2021.

Cover design by Charlene Kronstedt

Interior design by Exeter Premedia Services Private Ltd., Chennai, India

First published in 2021 by
Business Expert Press, LLC
222 East 46th Street, New York, NY 10017
www.businessexpertpress.com

ISBN-13: 978-1-95334-992-7 (paperback)
ISBN-13: 978-1-95334-993-4 (e-book)

Business Expert Press Financial Accounting, Auditing, and
Taxation Collection

Collection ISSN: 2151-2795 (print)
Collection ISSN: 2151-2817 (electronic)

First edition: 2021

10 9 8 7 6 5 4 3 2 1

Description

As an owner of a business or a manager, you will deal with numbers of various types. This book is written for those who may be responsible for, or are generally interested in, the activities of organizations but do not have the knowledge to interpret the financial information that is available.

The book identifies the types of organizations that generate financial information and explains how you can use it for your benefit. The early chapters focus on the information that is publicly available for large companies and demonstrate how to select and analyze the figures for decision making. The later chapters concentrate on the detailed management accounting information that is available internally for managers so that they can make decisions, investigate problems, and set performance targets. The final chapter, explores emerging and very pertinent issues such as "Can the organization obtain the basic resources to stay in business?" and "Are its activities harmful to the environment?"

Keywords

accounting equation; activity based management; balance sheet; budgetary control; cash flow statement; comparative analysis; data analytics; income statement; investment ratios; kaizen costing; key performance indicators; profit or loss account; same size analysis; standard costing; sustainability accounting; target costing; trend analysis; total quality management; vertical analysis; working capital

Contents

CHAPTER 1

Providers and Users of Financial Information

About This Chapter

Accounting is concerned with money in all its forms. Every day we have economic transactions. You buy gas, go out for lunch, get your iPad repaired, and worry about the strength of the dollar or pound against other currencies. Accounting recognizes these transactions and events, measures them, records them, and provides the information to those who want it and, more importantly, know how to use it.

The purpose of early forms of accounting was to provide business owners with financial information on the success of their business. The growth of different forms of business over the centuries has resulted in various types of accounting and there are also different types of providers and users. Businesses have grown both in the nature of their activities and also in the various groups interested in financial data. The potential users are tax authorities, banks and lenders, investors, managers, and the general public. As well as following their own pursuits, they can all have an interest in the financial performance and financial position of an organization.

Whether the organization is large or small, a profit or not-for-profit organization, it has to be managed efficiently. To be able to carry out their responsibilities, managers need financial information. The nature of that information will depend on the type of organization and the role of the manager. There are others who are also interested in information ranging from investors in the organization, competitor companies, and the general public who rely on these organizations for their pay or the services and the products they provide.

In this chapter, we will concentrate on the different types of information providers and the financial information they issue publicly. Much of this is required by regulation. We include in this chapter examples of the financial information from large organizations. This can be available either in the form of hard copy or on the websites of the organization. We also introduce the types of financial information that are intended specifically for those inside the organization and are not publicly available.

One word of caution. The financial reports that organizations issue can be extremely lengthy and complex. In this chapter, we give an overview of the financial information that you will find most interesting and useful. In Chapter 2, we demonstrate how to understand that information, and in Chapter 3, how to analyze it.

The Information Providers

Many different types of organizations have a public profile and ensure that information on what they are doing and how they are collecting and using finance is widely distributed. An example of such an organization is a not-for-profit organization such as a charity. We consider the financial information they provide in the next section before turning our attention to other types of organizations such as manufacturing and service companies. These provide similar types of information, as required by the regulations, but there are differences because of their type of business. They are, however, seeking to make a profit or to ensure that they have sufficient funds to continue their activities.

Most readers will know of the information given by the companies offering their shares to the public, but even small operations have to provide similar financial information to the taxation authorities, banks if they need a loan, and to managers.

Although organizations compile and issue their financial statements according to the regulations, unfortunately the regulations are not the same for every type of organization and in every country. Companies must comply with the regulations that come under the general heading of accounting standards in the country in which they are primarily based. Accounting standards set out principles, methods, and procedures that should be followed by a company in compiling its financial information.

The U.S. Developments

In the United States, the stock market crash of 1929 encouraged companies to issue an annual corporate financial report to their shareholders and other stakeholders who use it to evaluate financial performance. The Securities and Exchange Commission (SEC) was established in 1934 to remedy the poor corporate information that was available at that time (Galbraith 2009). The Financial Accounting Standards Board (FASB) in the United States was established in 1973 and is responsible to the Securities and Exchange Commission (SEC). The FASB for many years issued Statements of Financial Accounting Standards (SFASs) and now the FASB Accounting Standards Codification (ASC) is the official source of guidance.

The SEC requires publicly traded companies to file a Form 10-K, which provides a comprehensive review of a company's business and financial position as well as a report by an outside firm of auditors. In addition, companies are required to send an annual report to shareholders.

Comment letters are issued by the SEC's Division of Corporation Finance in response to a company's public filing. This letter, initially private, contains an itemized list of requests from the SEC. Each comment in the letter asks the filer to provide additional information, modify their submitted filing, or change the way they disclose in future filings. The filer must reply to each item in the comment letter. The SEC may then reply back with follow-up comments. This correspondence is later made public.

One area where companies may be tempted to make adjustments is in reporting revenue. In some companies, the directors' bonuses are based on revenue so one can appreciate the temptation to adjust it. A survey of comment letters issued by the SEC for 2018 and 2019 suggest that the SEC is looking at these practices more closely. The result has been that in some instances, the SEC urge companies to stop adjustments and to require greater disclosure by the companies (Linnane, McKenna, and Marriner 2019).

In June 2004, the SEC announced that it would publicly post all the comment letters, to give investors access to the information in those. An analysis of regulatory filings in May 2006 over the prior 12 months indicated that the SEC had not accomplished what it had said it would. The analysis found 212 companies that had reported receiving comment letters from the SEC, but only 21 letters for these companies were posted on the SEC's website. John W. White, the head of the Division of Corporation Finance, told the *New York Times* in 2006: "We have now resolved the hurdles of posting the information. We expect a significant number of new postings in the coming months."

Following the January 2018 collapse of construction and services business Carillion, it was reported that Carillion's auditor KPMG would have its role examined by the Financial Reporting Council (FRC). Two months later, the FRC's conduct committee announced an investigation into the conduct of the former Carillion finance directors Richard Adam and Zafar Khan.

A report by the Business and the Work and Pensions Select Committees into the collapse of Carillion, published on May 16, 2018, was critical of the FRC, describing it as feeble and timid, and of failing to follow up concerns in Carillion's 2015 accounts. Along with The Pensions Regulator, it was branded as "chronically passive." Welcoming the Government's review of the FRC's powers and effectiveness, the report said that changes to be a more aggressive and proactive regulator would need a significant shift in culture at the FRC itself.

Still under pressure to improve, in October 2018, the FRC proposed reforms, including banning from earning consultancy fees at businesses they audit, to tackle the underlying falling trust in business and the effectiveness of audit. In March 2019, the government announced that the FRC would be replaced by a new regulator, the Audit, Reporting and Governance Authority, with enhanced powers, in an effort to "change the culture" of the accounting sector.

The International Approach

When individual countries set their own accounting standards, the accounting techniques and methods of accounting can have strong national characteristics. The reasons for countries having different financial accounting and reporting regulations have been well researched (Frank 1979; Mueller 1967; Nair and Frank 1980; Nobes 1983). The consequence of countries setting their own individual regulations is the difficulty in comparing the financial performance of a company in one country with those of a company in another country.

In an attempt to remedy this problem, in 1973, several countries agreed to form the International Accounting Standards Committee (IASC), which was based in London, UK. The intention was that all companies would comply with the international standards regardless of their country of origin.

Progress was slow and in 1992 the standard setting bodies of Canada, the United Kingdom and the United States met to discuss ways for making quicker progress. The result was the formation of the International Accounting Standards Board (IASB) in 2001. Many countries require their companies to follow International Financial Reporting Standards (IFRSs) as issued by the International Accounting Standards Board (IASB) and it is claimed that the statements are better than when local company regulations were used.

Although many countries have adopted International Accounting Standards (now named International Financial Reporting Standards), the United States, which had invested considerable time and energy in the pursuit of internationalization, decided in 2014 not to proceed but to retain its own standard setting body. There were several factors that led to this decision and there are no indications that the United States will adopt international regulations (Hussey and Ong 2018).

Generally, unless you are conducting a very thorough investigation of a company's financial reports, you need not worry about differences in accounting regulations. However, do make certain when you are analyzing financial statements that the company states that it is complying with the regulations and whether they are U.S. or International Accounting Standards.

The UK Approach

The UK has adopted International Financial Reporting Standards but also has a Corporate Governance Code, which is a part of UK company law. This has a set of principles of good corporate governance aimed at companies listed on the London Stock Exchange. It is overseen by the Financial Reporting Council and its importance derives from the

Financial Conduct Authority's Listing Rules. Private companies are also encouraged to conform; however, there is no requirement for disclosure of compliance in private company accounts.

The Code adopts a principles-based approach in the sense that it provides general guidelines of best practice. In July 2018, the Financial Reporting Council released the new 2018 UK Corporate Governance Code, which is designed to build on the relationships between companies, shareholders, and stakeholders and make them key to long-term sustainable growth of the UK economy. To find out more visit the FRC website https://frc.org.uk/search?searchtext=misleading+financial+statements&searchmode=anyword&page=5

One significant change in the dissemination of corporate information that can assist you in obtaining financial details is the growth in the use of the Internet by companies. In the early days of use, it was argued that the Web is completely unregulated and the decision on what to disclose via the company's home page is entirely in the hands of management (Gowthorpe and Flynn 1997). Although that argument can still be applied in some instances, there has been a rapid growth in the companies' use of websites to get their message across and more robust information is given.

An early study (Hussey 2000) looked at disclosure developments from 1998 to 2000 of the top 100 UK companies. The results revealed that, in 1998, only nine of the companies did not have their own website and this had reduced to only four by the time of the 2000 survey.

By 2000, more companies had a website and 95 provided some financial information. Of the 63 companies using their website in March 1998, the majority of disclosures were in standard web page format. 24 companies supplied Adobe Acrobat files on their web page, which, in most cases, exactly mirrored the published document. By the year 2000, portable document format (pdf) was being used by 85 percent of the companies providing financial information.

Another later study (Pendley and Rai 2008) concluded that developments in technology can present problems in the nature and quality of information provided. The authors took a sample of the websites of the U.S. companies during the period 2006 to 2007. They found a major structural change in the method used to deliver online financial reports. This change involves the increased use of third-party outsourcing services in the delivery of online financial information.

Doubts on the possible quality of financial information on websites was confirmed by an analysis of websites of 58 JSE-listed companies in 2012 and 2015. Their conclusion was that disclosure behavior overall had improved over the period of their sample, especially regarding extra content and technological features. The authors of the study argued that technology may be an enabler of general website usability, but not necessarily for financial reports (Nel and Esterhuyse 2019).

As a final word, we would emphasize that financial information on websites can differ from country to country and over time. The findings of one study showed that economic development is an important factor determining the websites' financial disclosure practices and differences (Khoufia and Khrifech 2018). The position is improving as increasingly countries are requiring companies to file their financial information using eXtensible Business Reporting Language (XBRL). This format allows an analysis of large amounts of financial information and eases comparisons to statements filed using other formats.

Although the studies we have referred to have expressed a need for caution when using information from websites, we would not wish to overstate the dangers. If you are collecting financial information from websites, then extract the *audited* financial statements. In Chapters 2 and 3, we explain how you can conduct your own analysis and draw your own conclusions.

The Main Financial Statements

If you obtain the annual report and accounts of a company, you may well be overwhelmed by the size of it and the substantial volume of information given. Do not despair! We are going to concentrate on the three main financial statements, which every company produces and are important to your decision making on the company.

Because of the different types of companies and different accounting standards used by the United States and internationally, the titles given to the statements may be different. Also, companies that are not listed on a Stock Exchange may use other titles. With small organizations only giving the information to the owners and the taxation authorities, slightly different titles may be used. Do not worry as in Chapter 2 we provide a terminology explaining the different terms. At this stage, we give the most frequently used titles.

These statements are as follows:

Earnings Statement/Income Statement/Profit Statement

This statement focuses on the financial performance of an organization. At its simplest, it shows the value of the sales made in the financial period, the costs that were incurred and the profit or loss. The document may also have the term "Consolidated" as part of the headings. This means that it is the profit results of several companies in a group of companies and the financial statement is giving the total picture. If a financial statement has the words "Comprehensive," then take care. This is a term we explain fully in Chapter 2.

Statement of Financial Position (The Balance Sheet)

The statement is similar to a snapshot of the business at one point in time showing what it owns (assets) and what it owes (liabilities). The total of the assets will be the same as the total of the liabilities plus the equity being the investment by the owners, hence the term "Balance Sheet." The trend is to use the longer "Statement" description, although smaller companies frequently use the term Balance Sheet.

Cash Flow Statement

We explain in Chapter 2 that profit and cash are not the same thing. A company may make a profit but it can still go bankrupt! It is obviously important that you appreciate the difference between profit and cash when you are evaluating the performance of an organization.

In the next section, we show some large company examples of the three above main financial statements. Remember that these are organizations making a public financial statement. You will find that smaller companies and the Mom and Pop stores do not have the same volume of information.

Examples from Information Providers

Not-for-Profit-Entities

We briefly include not-for profit-entities in our explanations because they can be very large organizations and include charities, foundations, colleges and universities, health care providers, cultural institutions, religious organizations, and trade associations. With these entities, fund raising can be substantial and required not only to provide their services but to pay employees and other organizational costs. The managers and those associated with these organizations have to make tough decisions and need financial information to do so.

There are researches that have been conducted into the financial information required of, and provided by not-for-profit entities, many years ago. A study by Daniels, Braswell, and Beeler (2010) explored the accounting and financial reporting of the first municipal orphanage in America—the Charleston Orphan House. This was established in 1790 by the city and was required to keep a book of fair and regular accounts of all the receipts and expenditures, "which will be subject at all times to the inspection of the Commissioners."

We have moved some distance away from the above example, but questions have been raised on the reliability of charities' financial statements. One study (Burks 2015) of a sample of 5,511 audited financial statements, predominantly from the years 2006 to 2010, found that public charities had a 60 percent higher rate of errors than that of publicly traded corporations, and almost twice as high as that of similar-sized corporations. Most of the errors were those of omission, that is, failing to recognize certain items and it is not claimed that fraud was taking place.

There are now even more regulations concerning the financial management of not-for-profit organizations. This may improve the reliability of financial statements but also add further costs. With major not-for profit organizations, one can usually have confidence in the financial information that is being given. In 2016, the Financial Accounting

Standards Board (FASB) in the United States issued Accounting Standards Update (ASU) No. 2016-14, which concerned the presentation of financial statements by not-for-profit entities. A useful explanation and discussion of these requirements are provided by Fitzsimons, McCarthy, and Silliman (2018).

Not-for-profit organizations are an important part of our economy and play a significant role in all our daily lives. As an example of the role they play in our society, we show an extract from the 2019 annual report from the charity "Feeding America." We include only the part that shows the finance received from public support, such as fund raising and donated goods and the additional revenue that has been generated.

Feeding America

https://feedingamerica.org/about-us/financials

This year, the Feeding America network helped provide a record 4.3 billion meals to people facing hunger. Thanks to supporters like you, struggling families nationwide are receiving groceries from their local food pantry, served by a Feeding America member food bank.

Statement of Activities

OPERATING ACTIVITIES		
PUBLIC SUPPORT AND REVENUE		
PUBLIC SUPPORT	2018	2017
Fundraising	$163,292	$148,166
Donated goods and services	2,637,558	2,543,586
TOTAL PUBLIC SUPPORT	2,800,850	2,691,752

REVENUE		
Food procurement revenue	$70,889	$65,957
Other revenue	7,909	8,070
TOTAL PUBLIC SUPPORT AND REVENUE	$2,879,648	$2,765,779

EXPENSES		
PROGRAM SERVICES	2018	2017
Member services	$70,967	$53,059
Food procurement	2,753,823	2,632,594
Public awareness and education	6,695	5,552
Policy and advocacy	2,526	1,972
Programs	4,380	4,015
Research and analysis	3,476	3,153
TOTAL PROGRAM SERVICES	2,841,867	2,700,345

SUPPORTING SERVICES		
Management and general	$11,987	$8,104
Fund development	27,079	25,884
TOTAL SUPPORTING SERVICES	39,066	33,988
TOTAL EXPENSES	$2,880,933	$2,734,333

This small extract from a substantial amount of information on their website informs us of the total revenue they have received from the public and how those funds have been used. We will see similar statements for companies that are listed on a stock exchange, and in the next section, we concentrate on the Income Statement, which shows how any profits have been generated.

Income Statement

Companies that are manufacturing have products they both make and sell. On their income statement, we expect to see a sales figure and also some details of all the costs they have incurred. If the figure for sales is higher than the costs, we end up with a profit, although it may be labeled as "earnings" on the financial statement. We show the Income Statement below for Volkswagen.

The Volkswagen Example

https://volkswagenag.com › Investor Relations › news-and-publications

Income Statement			
€ million	Note	2018	2017
1 Prior-year figures adjusted			
Sales revenue	1	235,849	229,550
Cost of sales	2	−189,500	−186,001
Gross result		46,350	43,549
Distribution expenses	3	−20,510	−20,859
Administrative expenses	4	−8,819	−8,126
Other operating income	5	11,631	11,514
Other operating expenses	6	−14,731	−12,259
Operating result		13,920	13,818
Share of the result of equity-accounted investments	7	3,369	3,482
Interest income	8	967	951
Interest expenses	8	−1,547	−2,317
Other financial result	9	−1,066	−2,262
Financial result		1,723	−146
Earnings before tax		15,643	13,67

The income statement, as with all the companies, shows the sales revenue and deducts all the costs incurred in generating that revenue. Also, in
the document, the company states the basis for preparing the statement.
The company complied with international accounting standards as stated
in the following paragraph.

"In accordance with Regulation No. 1606/2002 of the European
Parliament and of the Council, Volkswagen AG prepared its consolidated
financial statements for 2018 in compliance with the International Financial Reporting Standards (IFRSs), as adopted by the European Union.
We have complied with all the IFRSs adopted by the EU and required to
be applied."

Statement of Financial Position

The balance sheet or statement of financial position can be thought of as
a snapshot in one point of time. Depending on the type of company, the
balance sheet may show different items but the total value of everything
it owns (its assets) must be the same as everything it owes (liabilities) plus

the owner's interests—the equity. The example below is from Walmart, which is a retailing company and, at its simplest, buys and sells goods. With manufacturing companies, you will see some different individual items but the overall purpose of the financial statement is the same. It demonstrates the financial position of the company at a particular date.

The Walmart Example

https://s2.q4cdn.com › files › doc_financials › WMT-2018_Annual-Report

This is a U.S. company, so it lodges what is known as a form 10K with the Securities and Exchange Commission (SEC). This is a public document. We have extracted the "Consolidated Balance Sheet as of January 31, 2018" but we are concentrating only on the figures for 2018 for clarity, although data for the previous year was given. When we discuss the analysis of financial statements in the next chapter, we emphasize that an analysis that covers several years is the most helpful for making decisions rather than the figures for only one year.

Report of Independent Registered Public Accounting Firm

To the Shareholders and the Board of Directors of Walmart Inc.

Opinion on the Financial Statements

We have audited the accompanying consolidated balance sheets of Walmart Inc. (the Company) as of January 31, 2018 and 2017, the related consolidated statements of income, comprehensive income, shareholders' equity and cash flows for each of the three years in the period ended January 31, 2018, and the related notes (collectively referred to as the consolidated financial statements).

In our opinion, the consolidated financial statements present fairly, in all material respects, the financial position of the Company at January 31, 2018 and 2017, and the results of its operations and its cash flows for each of the three years in the period ended January 31, 2018, in conformity with U.S. generally accepted accounting principles.

Walmart Inc. Consolidated Balance Sheets as of January 31	
	(Amounts in millions) **2018**
Current assets:	
Cash and cash equivalents	6,756
Receivables, net	5,614
Inventories	43,783
Prepaid expenses and other	3,511
Total current assets	59,664
Property and equipment:	
Property and equipment	185,154
Less accumulated depreciation	(77,479)
Property and equipment, net	107,675
Property under capital lease and financing obligations:	
Property under capital lease and financing obligations	12,703
Less accumulated amortization	(5,560)
Property under capital lease and financing obligations, net	7,143
Goodwill	18,242
Other assets and deferred charges	11,798
Total assets	204,522
LIABILITIES AND EQUITY	
Current liabilities:	
Short-term borrowings	5,257
Accounts payable	46,092
Accrued liabilities	22,122
Accrued income taxes	645
Long-term debt due within one year	3,738
Capital lease and financing obligations due within one year	667
Total current liabilities	78,521
Long-term debt	30,045
Long-term capital lease and financing obligations	6,780
Deferred income taxes and other	8,354
Commitments and contingencies	
Equity:	
Common stock	295
Capital in excess of par value	2,648
Retained earnings	85,107

Accumulated other comprehensive loss	(10,181)
Total Walmart shareholders' equity	77,869
Noncontrolling interest	2,953
Total equity	80,822
Total liabilities and equity	204,522

Because of the nature of its business, Walmart will have some different items on its balance sheet than other companies. However, it is basically the same as all balance sheets and the amount shown for total assets is the same as the amount for total liabilities and equity, which represents the investment by shareholders. In other words, the balance sheet balances. Equity represents shareholders' investment in the company. It is important to remember that it is the shareholders that own the listed company and the balance sheet recognizes this. Remember, however, that the amount shown on the balance sheet does not usually match the quoted value of shares listed on a stock exchange.

Cash Flow Statement

This is one of the most recent main financial statement for companies to disclose. The problem we had was that a few rogue companies were showing profits in their income statement but still becoming bankrupt. As we explain fully in the next chapter, profit is not the same as cash. The users of financial information need to know what the cash position is and this statement provides the information.

The Unilever Example

This company complies with the International Financial Reporting Standards (IFRSs) and the Netherlands Civil Code. It also uses the phrase "true and fair view," which you will not find in statements complying with the U.S. regulation. For our purposes, if we see that phrase in the Auditors' Report, we can have confidence that the company has followed the rules. We have extracted from the original document that shows only the amounts for 2018, starting with the net cash flow from operating activities.

Auditors are expected to give an opinion on the financial statements and we show below part of that opinion.

In our opinion:

- the accompanying Consolidated Financial Statements give a true and fair view of the financial position of the Group as at 31 December 2018 and of its result and its cash flows for the year then ended in accordance with International Financial Reporting Standards as adopted by the European Union (IFRS as adopted by the EU) and with Part 9 of Book 2 of the Netherlands Civil Code; and
- the accompanying NV Company Accounts give a true and fair view of the financial position of Unilever N.V. as at 31 December 2018 and of its result for 2018 in accordance with United Kingdom accounting standards, including FRS 101 Reduced Disclosure Framework and Part 9 of Book 2 of the Netherlands Civil Code.

UNILEVER GROUP CONTINUED	
CONSOLIDATED CASH FLOW STATEMENT	
for the year ended December 31	
	€ million
	2018
Net cash flow from operating activities	6,753
Interest received	110
Purchase of intangible assets	(203)
Purchase of property, plant and equipment	(1,329)
Disposal of property, plant and equipment	108
Acquisition of group companies, joint ventures and associates	(1,336)
Disposal of group companies, joint ventures and associates	7,093
Acquisition of other non-current investments	(94)
Disposal of other non-current investments	151
Dividends from joint ventures, associates and other non-current investments	154
(Purchase)/sale of financial assets	(10)
Net cash flow (used in)/from investing activities	4,644
Dividends paid on ordinary share capital	(4,066)

Interest and preference dividends paid	(477)
Net change in short-term borrowings	(4,026)
Additional financial liabilities	10,595
Repayment of financial liabilities	(6,594)
Capital element of finance lease rental payments	(10)
Repurchase of shares	(6,020)
Other movements on treasury shares	(257)
Other financing activities	(693)
Net cash flow (used in)/from financing activities	**(11,548)**
Net increase/(decrease) in cash and cash equivalents	**(151)**
Cash and cash equivalents at the beginning of the year	**3,169**
Effect of foreign exchange rate changes	72
Cash and cash equivalents at the end of the year 17A	**3,090**

The examples of the three key financial statements we have shown above are from very large companies, so they contain substantial amounts of information. This can be very intimidating. However, when we discuss analyzing the financial statements in Chapter 2, we explain the main items of information you can extract from the financial statements to enable you to analyze the performance of the company.

Users of Financial Information

The Information Needs

All types of organizations need financial information to ensure that they are managed effectively. There are also many others, both within and outside the organization, interested in its activities. The nature of the organization will determine who is entitled legally to receive financial information and the scope and detail of that information.

Managers within the organization will need information to do their job. The extent and nature of that information will depend on the responsibilities of the manager. The top person will require a complete financial picture, whereas those managers with lesser responsibilities may only receive part of the information. However, even where an organization is not legally required to give information, many do so to all of their employees.

The types of information that a manager may require is likely to be very detailed, is relevant to only one part of the organization, and is required at least monthly and sometimes monthly or weekly. This is costing or management accounting information and we explain this type of information and how to analyze it in Chapter 4.

There are other seekers of financial information that have no legal rights to such information but will require it for several purposes. The best example is a bank or other lenders of finance. They are highly unlikely to agree to any form of loan unless they have a complete picture of the organization's financial strengths and weaknesses. As far as legal rights are concerned, the tax authorities must be at the top of the list. In every country, the tax authorities have full access to the financial records.

The reason for you seeking information will determine your search strategy. If you are specifically interested in the financial performance and financial strength of a company, you will be most interested in the annual report and accounts. This includes the main financial statements and we explain how to understand and analyze these in Chapter 2. If you are more interested in obtaining some general information on what the company does, you will find information on this in the annual report, but we recommend conducting some financial analysis to support any conclusions you are making.

An early study (Smith and Taffler 1995) noted that although annual reports were incorporating substantial narrative information, many did not correspond with the actual financial results and tended to use an unduly optimistic tone likely to mislead the user of such statements. More recently, it has been argued that narrative reporting can be misleading, unstructured, incomparable and may be more than an outlet for corporate image building (Mishra and Haldar 2019). Our advice is to be cautious when reading the narrative information and to apply the analysis we demonstrate in Chapter 2.

Sources of Financial Information

Above we showed the financial statements from some international companies. These are of interest to all types of users of corporate information. If you are seeking a U.S. source of information on a company, we suggest you visit EDGAR. This is the Electronic Data Gathering, Analysis, and Retrieval system used at the U.S. Securities and Exchange Commission (SEC) for companies and others who are required by law to file information with the SEC. The system has millions of company and individual filings and processes about 3,000 filings per day, serves up to 3,000 terabytes of data to the public annually, and accommodates 40,000 new filers per year on average. The best news is that your access to Edgar's database is free.

In the UK, company information can be obtained from Companies House: https://gov.uk/get-information-about-a-company. There is no charge for the information and you can obtain some details about a company including:

- company information, for example, registered address and date of incorporation
- current and resigned officers
- document images
- mortgage charge data
- previous company names
- insolvency information

Before you launch on an examination of an organization's financial statements, it is important to recognize that different countries may have their own set of regulations that detail what financial information an organization should make public and how the accounting standards should be set.

For many years, individual countries set their own accounting rules. This made international business difficult and, from 1973, various attempts were made to establish international financial regulations. Progress was made and now the International Accounting Standards Board sets International Financial Reporting Standards. However, it is individual countries that decide whether they should adopt such standards and to what extent.

Many countries have adopted international standards but, after several years of discussion and debate, the United States decided to maintain responsibility for its own standards (Hussey and Ong 2018). To make international comparisons even more difficult, it has been argued that because of cultural differences, there are varying degrees of IFRS acceptance: some countries adopt the full set of IFRS, while others only accept certain standards (Ward and Lowe 2017).

Corporate Examples

It is essential that before you commence analyzing the financial statements of any company, you know the accounting regulations it is following. We show the statements made by four different companies so that you are prepared for the analysis we discuss in Chapter 2.

Diageo plc—U.K. Company IFRS Example

This company's products are sold in more than 180 countries around the world and include such brands as Johnnie Walker, Smirnoff, Captain Morgan, Baileys, and Guinness. On page 94 of the 164-page annual report for 2018, it states:

> The financial statements of the group are prepared in accordance with International Financial Reporting Standards (IFRS) as adopted for use in the European Union (EU) and as issued by the International Accounting Standards Board

Rosneft Oil—Russian Company IFRS Example

This company conducts exploration and appraisal of hydrocarbon fields, production of *oil*, gas, and gas condensate, offshore field development projects, feedstock processing, sales of *oil*, gas, and refined products in the territory of Russia and abroad. Page 273 of 392 pages of annual report for 2018 states:

> The accompanying consolidated financial statements present fairly, in all material respects, the consolidated financial position of the Company as at 31 December 2018 and its consolidated financial performance and its consolidated cash flows for the year then ended in accordance with International Financial Reporting Standards (IFRSs).

Walmart U.S. Page 54 of 100 Pages

Walmart Inc. is an American multinational retail corporation. Walmart is the world's largest company by revenue, with US $514.405 billion, in 2019 and is the largest private employer in the world with 2.2 million employees. Page 54 of 100 pages in the annual report for 2019 states:

> In our opinion, the consolidated financial statements present fairly, in all material respects, the financial position of the Company at January 31, 2019 and 2018, and the results of its operations and its cash flows for each of the three years in the period ended January 31, 2019, in conformity with U.S. generally accepted accounting principles.

George Weston Ltd

This is a Canadian public company, founded in 1882. George Weston has three operating segments: Loblaw Companies Limited, Canada's largest food and drug retailer and a provider of financial services, Choice Properties Real Estate Investment Trust, Canada's largest and preeminent diversified REIT, and Weston Foods, one of North America's leading producers of quality baked goods. Page 5 of 178 pages states:

> The Company's audited annual consolidated financial statements and the accompanying notes for the year ended December 31, 2019 have been prepared in accordance with International Financial Reporting Standards ("IFRS" or "GAAP") as issued by the International Accounting Standards Board ("IASB").

The term "GAAP" stands for Generally Accepted Accounting Principles.

You will note that, although George Weston is a Canadian company, and thus a neighbor of the United States, it follows International Accounting Standards, which is required in that country.

The rule is to check the annual report that will state which accounting standards the company follows.

You do not need to know the regulations in detail. This would be a mammoth task. However, if you find your analysis provides unexpected or inexplicable results, it is a good plan to examine the possible ratio that is causing the problems.

Types of Financial Information

Accounting has a long history if one accepts the broad definition of keeping records of economic activities. There is evidence that the practice can be traced back to thousands of years (Robson 1943). A critical milestone in accounting was the publication in Venice in 1494 of Pacioli's Summa de Arithmetica Geometria Proportioni et Proportionalita. It is argued that this guide to bookkeeping revolutionized commerce throughout Europe and accountants apply the same principles today (Sangster and Scataglinibelghitar 2010).

There have been many changes in accounting over the last 500 years. The developments over that time in the UK have been documented (Parker and Yarney 1994) and those with a shorter history in the United States (Previts and Marino 1998). Accounting records are a source of historical practices and provide information on changes in accounting applications, organizational structures, and management practices. Most of the early history is concerned with accounting information that is intended for the direct owners of a business. Not only would they want to know whether the business was profitable on a yearly basis, but they would also wish to scrutinize the money they were owed and the money they owed to others. As businesses became larger, more complex, and with managers in charge of daily operations, so the nature of the accounting information changed.

Accounting became divided into two disciplines. Financial accounting that focuses on the entire organization and management accounting, also known as cost accounting, which concentrates on different activities within the organization. Certainly, managers are interested in the total financial activities of the organization, but also the owners and other bodies such as banks that are lending money to the organization and, of course, the tax authorities. For the running of the organization on a daily basis, managers required detailed information on the costs for which they are responsible. This information is provided by management accounting which is not normally given to those outside of the organization. We discuss these two different types of accounting in the following sections.

Financial Accounting

Most, if not all, educational courses and books on accounting start with explanations of financial accounting rather than management accounting. This is because it is the foundation for running a business and is focused on the entire organization. Everyone who has some connection with a business has an interest in its financial performance. Questions such as "How much profit did it make" and "Will it go bankrupt" are answered by financial accounting.

What financial accounting provides is information in the form of structured financial statements for a period of time. At least for one year and often half-yearly or quarterly. Small businesses, whether they are one person businesses or a relatively few employees, do not produce complex financial statements. The statements will be drawn up in accordance with accounting practices but there are few external requirements. Tax authorities will want to see them and the bank manager will be interested if you are seeking a loan, but the most interested people are the owners and those wishing, for various reasons, to understand the financial position and progress of the organizations.

For small businesses, there are three main financial statements:

A Cash Statement

This will show the actual cash movements in and out for a period of time. It does not show the amount of profit the company has made. The usual format would be:

- Cash Inflows, which would usually be the cash that the company has received from the sales it has made
- Cash payments that have been made for such items as wages, materials, rent, power, and similar cash outlays so that the business can operate

Although the term "cash" is used, the statement also recognizes other forms of receipts and payments such as checks and bank drafts.

An Income (Profit) Statement

Sometimes known as the profit or loss, as this is essentially an output from a company's accounting system. For example, if you bought and paid for an item on January 1 for $3000 and sold it at the end of January for $3500, you will have made $500 profit. It may be that you have not yet received payment, but in accounting terms, you have made a profit. If you have not yet paid for the item, in accounting terms, you have made a profit even if you do not have the cash. The profit statement shows the amount of profit made over a period of time. It does not show movements of cash in and out of the business. It does not show the amount of cash the business has. That information is given in the balance sheet.

Unfortunately, the terminology used in the Profit or Income Statement can vary depending on the country and the standards with which it is complying. Even with countries applying International Accounting Standard, there can be variations in the terms and methods used. It has been pointed out that "unrealistic for a single set of standards to be accepted and implemented in a wholly uniform manner to produce innately comparable financial statements" (Ward and Lowe 2017). In the United States, the tendency is to use the terms Earnings or Income Statement.

These variations in terminology and format on the financial statement should not cause you any problems. Usually, you can take the first amount on the statement and that will be the business generated in the financial period. This amount will be followed by all the costs to give the income or profit.

A Balance Sheet

Sometimes referred to as a statement of financial position, it is like a snapshot of the business. It shows what the business owns and what it owes at one point in time. What a business owns is known as assets. What a business owes is known as liabilities. There will have been an investment in the business by the owners and this is known as capital or equity, and with companies, it will be the shareholdings. The basis of a balance sheet is the accounting equation:

$$Assets = Capital + Liabilities$$

The accounting equation must balance. If the capital and liabilities are higher than the assets, the business is bankrupt.

For large companies, the financial information is usually publicly available in their annual report or on their website. The content of the financial statements is highly regulated so you can rely on them. For smaller companies, you may have to request the information. If you do obtain it, they should be approved by a firm of accountants or, at least, the taxation authorities should have seen them.

The Full Financial Package

We have explained the three main financial statements. For a business of any size, these should be available. When we start looking at larger businesses, particularly those that have investors, we will find much more information. This may be available as a printed document but with major companies, there is a mass of information on their website.

Below we show the contents page from the annual report of **General Motors Company**, commonly referred to as **GM**. It is an American multinational corporation headquartered in Detroit that designs, manufactures, markets, and distributes vehicles and vehicle parts, and sells financial services, with global headquarters in Detroit's Renaissance Center. As with other U.S. companies, it must file certain information with the Securities and Exchange Commission. We show below the contents page of the annual report filed for 2018, which is available on their website (https://investor.gm.com/investor-relations).

INDEX

Page

PART I

Item 1. Business Item

1A. Risk Factors

Item 1B. Unresolved Staff Comments Item

2. Properties Item 3. Legal Proceedings

Item 4. Mine Safety Disclosures

PART II

Item 5. Market for Registrant's Common Equity, Related Stockholder Matters and Issuer Purchases of Equity Securities

Item 7. Management's Discussion and Analysis of Financial Condition and Results of Operations Item

7A. Quantitative and Qualitative Disclosures About Market Risk

Item 8. Financial Statements and Supplementary Data

Consolidated Income Statements

Consolidated Statements of Comprehensive

Consolidated Balance Sheets

Consolidated Statements of Cash Flows

Consolidated Statements of Equity

Notes to Consolidated Financial Statements

PART III

Item 10. Directors, Executive Officers and Corporate Governance

Item 11. Executive Compensation

Item 12. Security Ownership of Certain Beneficial Owners and Management and Related Stockholder Matters

Item 13. Certain Relationships and Related Transactions and Director Independence

Item 14. Principal Accountant Fees and Services

PART IV

Item 15. Exhibits

Item 16. Form 10-K Summary

This report is 104 pages in length and it is not one of the longest reports issued by companies. In fact, annual reports issued by companies have grown in length in recent years (Hussey and Ong 2018). It is also not the only data that is made publicly available by General Motors. If you visit the website, you can be overwhelmed by the amount of information available.

However, in this book, we concentrate on the three main financial statements that should be shown by every company in the world that has its shares listed on a Stock Exchange or is subject to any regulations that require disclosure of financial information. Most importantly, the owners and managers of the business require the information contained on these three financial statements to successfully run the business. In Chapters 2 and 3, we will explain and illustrate how you can use the information contained in these three statements.

Management Accounting

Although management accounting came many years after financial accounting, it has a lengthy history and it started with the title "cost accounting." If we consider the UK, a form of management accounting that can be traced from the later Middle Ages (Boyns and Edwards 2013). It is argued that the nature of the discipline changed in the 1970s because of the scale and nature of the changes in management accounting theories and practices.

The value of management accounting is easy to appreciate. Well managed organizations require information more frequently and for it to be more detailed than provided by the annual financial statements. To satisfy this need, cost accounting, also known as management accounting, was developed. The information generated is given to internal managers. This may be on a monthly, weekly, or in some instances on a daily basis. The information is not usually made available to those outside the organization, although competitors would be very interested in seeing it.

Management accounting, as with financial accounting, uses the "accruals" concept of accounting for transactions. This means that transactions are recognized when they take place and not when cash is received or paid, although the events may be simultaneous such as when you pay at the checkout at a supermarket.

An organization chooses whether to have a management accounting system and the type of system. It should serve the useful purpose of providing managers with information so that they can carry out their responsibilities and contribute to the success of the organization. In a small business, the owner may be the only "manager." The management accounting system is likely to be rudimentary and may be little more than the financial accounting system with some important details added. The owner is likely to make all the decisions, and the performance measure will be of the entire business and not different parts of it. If there are "managers," their role may be simply in following the instructions of the owner.

In a large business, a center or department is usually under the control of an accounting manager who will have the responsibility for the resources used. One common need of managers is to know what "something" costs and the reason. Unfortunately, the term "cost" is slippery and defies one simple explanation. The "something" for which managers wish to know the cost is usually a center or department or a cost unit. It may even be a single item.

In addition to being precise as to what is being costed, it is important to specify the nature of the cost. It may be the cost of labor and material used in manufacturing a product. It could be the cost of maintenance or administrative overheads or the cost of running a machine on a particular piece of work. To complicate matters, the "cost" for a particular unit of production or service can change depending on the level of activity and we will discuss this later in Chapter 3.

Knowing the actual cost is a start but managerial and organizational performance is improved if control is exercised by comparing this actual cost with some form of benchmark or standard and investigating differences. This enables managers to plan future activities, monitor and control the results, evaluate performance, and make decisions.

The actual cost could be compared to:

- Previous costs for the same activity. This will show whether we did better or worse than for a prior period of time. Unfortunately, all the errors and deficiencies in incurring the previous cost may obscure whether the performance has improved.

- Costs for alternative courses of action. This could range from outsourcing or switching to different products or processes.
- Planned costs, which will involve the careful calculation of predetermined costs for a specific period of time.
- The costs incurred by external organizations for the same activity. This information may be difficult to acquire but strategic competitiveness should be a part of an organization's portfolio.

Conclusions

In this introductory chapter, we have set the scene for applying accounting literacy for business success. We have explained that organizations need financial information to operate efficiently. We have also explained that there are many users of a company's financial information. All of us are acquainted with the demands of tax authorities but there are others who want more detailed information. There are the lenders, such as banks and others, who have different forms of relationship with a company. For example, suppliers need to know that they are going to be paid and whether the company will stay in business and thus offer further trade.

The information requirements of these groups can usually be met by a company's financial information system and the disclosures contained in the three main financial statements: the income statement, the balance sheet, and the cash flow statement. In Chapter 2, we explain how financial accounting analysis based on these three financial statements can be used to provide valuable insights into a company's performance.

There is also a financial information need by those responsible for running the business. Information on how much a product or process costs and what should it have cost are essential for effective management. In Chapter 4, we explain the types of management accounting techniques, and in Chapter 5, how these can be successfully applied. The final chapter, Chapter 6, takes a broader view and discusses the effects of change and developments that are taking place.

Action Plan

You will find at this stage it is helpful to determine the reason you want financial information. Possible reasons are:

1. You work for the company and want to know how successful it is and whether this has an impact on your own job.
2. You own the company and need to make decisions that have potential financial consequences.
3. You have purchased, or intend to purchase, shares in a company and wish to know whether it is a shrewd investment.
4. You are a supplier or customer of the company and wish to know how stable it is.
5. General interest

In the subsequent chapters, you will find explanations of different types of financial information. An organization generates a significant amount of financial information for different purposes. Having identified your reason for wanting such information, you will appreciate the value of specific information.

CHAPTER 2

Examining Financial Statements

About This Chapter

You will find that a company's annual report, as discussed in Chapter 1, whether printed or on a company website, contains a substantial amount of information. There may be a mixture of financial information as well as such issues as sustainability and key performance indicators. We discuss these topics in Chapter 6.

It is easy to be overwhelmed by the amount of information. So, in this chapter, we introduce the three main financial statements we discussed in Chapter 1. These are:

- An Income Statement also known as a Statement of Financial Performance or as a Profit Statement
- Balance sheet also known as a Statement of Financial Position
- Cash Statement

These statements in a company's annual report will be accompanied by many pages of explanation of the figures, which may be difficult to understand. However, by extracting the key figures from the financial statements, you can calculate ratios, which give you an insight into an organization's financial position and performance irrespective of any gloss that may be put on by the directors of the company.

Although we refer to a company's annual report as these are usually available and reliable, you will find that even small organizations collect similar information. They need to know what profit or loss they made, what they own and owe, and how much cash they have. The knowledge gained from this book will enable you to assess the success or otherwise of any size or type of organization. It will also help you to decide on what actions, if any, you need to take to generate business success.

To gain a full understanding of a company's financial performance and financial position, you need comparators. This may be the information from other companies or for the same company over several years. You will find that companies make public the three main financial statements we have identified above not only for the current year, but also for previous years.

We gave examples from company's annual financial reports in the first chapter. Until you are familiar with these documents, the amount of information they contain can be daunting, so we start this chapter with a brief Terminology section. This will help you with some of the accounting jargon. This is followed by a section about the types of information you can expect to find in a company's full annual report and accounts, frequently called the Corporate Report.

The major part of the chapter concentrates on the three main financial statements. We will be giving our attention to for-profit organizations, but it is convincingly argued that not-for-profit organizations can also make use of certain ratios to judge the effectiveness of their activities (Cashwell, Copley, and Dugan 2019). Having described the three main financial statements, we have drafted some fictitious business examples and demonstrate how you can calculate ratios to analyze financial success or otherwise.

Terminology

The terminology used in financial statements issued by companies whose shares are listed on a Stock Exchange can be intimidating. These financial statements are regulated by standard setters. It is argued that the standards issued by the Financial Accounting Standards Board in the United States and the International Accounting Standards Board have significant differences there and also have differences with the Internal Revenue Code in many countries (Sedki, Posada, and Pruske 2018).

Fortunately, with smaller organizations, the accounting description of their business is much shorter and simpler. However, be cautious with your analysis and, if examining listed companies, search the financial press for opinions and comment.

Balance Sheet. This is like a financial snapshot of the organization at one particular date usually the last day of its financial year. The total amount of all its assets balance with the total amount it owes.

Comprehensive Income Statement. This can be considered as the organization's total wealth at the end of the financial period less its wealth at the beginning of the period.

Earnings is usually meant to mean a company's after-tax income. Investors usually use this as a measure of a company's possible profitability in the long term.

Earnings before interest and tax (EBIT). This statement shows exactly what its name states and is usually looked at closely by shareholders.

Earnings Statement. See profit statement.

Equity is the value that the owners, usually the shareholders put on a business. It is calculated by deducting the liabilities of a company from its assets. The market value of equity is based on the current share price of the company.

Income Statement. Generally, this can be considered as very similar to the Profit or Loss Statement.

Profit or Loss Statement. This shows the revenue for the financial period less the costs incurred in generating that income. If the sales are higher than the costs, there is a profit. Remember that this is not a cash statement.

Profit or Loss Account. You may find small businesses tending to use this term because it is an output from their method of accounting. It shows the amount received for its sales and services for the current year and the costs incurred. Remember this is not a cash statement.

The Annual Report

All sizes and types of organizations draw up financial statements, at least annually. Managers need to know their financial performance and position. Employees, customers, and suppliers can be affected by the annual financial result. Certainly, the taxation authorities will need to assess what are in the results for them to have their share of the profits. With larger companies, one can expect that there are lenders and investors who are very keen to see the figures.

With large companies, the amount of information provided can be overwhelming and can be divided into two main types. The information that a company is required by regulations to make public and that information a company voluntarily offers for various reasons. Below we show the annual report contents for Proctor and Gamble. This report is approximately 80 pages in length and the company also has a website that contains substantial information.

Proctor and Gamble. Annual Report 2019

Letter to Shareowners i
P&G's 10-Category Portfolio ii
Noticeable Superiority vi
Constructive Disruption x
Form 10-K xv
Company and
Shareholder Information 73
Measures Not Defined by
U.S. GAAP 74
Company Leadership 76
Board of Directors 77
Recognition and Commitments 78
Citizenship at P&G Inside Back Cover

The Form 10-K noted above is an annual report required by the U.S. Securities and Exchange Commission to be filed by public companies. Federal laws state that public companies must provide information on an ongoing basis and submit annual reports on Form 10-K, quarterly reports on Form 10-Q, and current reports on Form 8-K .

Form 10-K provides a comprehensive overview of the company's business and financial condition and includes comments from independent auditors. The annual report on Form 10-K is frequently distinct from the Annual Report to Shareholders, which companies must send to its shareholders when it holds an annual meeting to elect directors. If you wish to study a particular company's Form 10-K filings, your free access is the SEC's Edgar database (https://sec.gov/edgar.shtml).

You will note that in addition to Form 10-K, which is a required disclosure, the company includes other information. One item is "Measures Not Defined by U.S. GAAP." In other words, there are no regulations that require this disclosure. Such information could be useful but the reader should take care to ensure that they understand the information and the caution attached to it.

With most companies, a printed annual report is easily available. You will find that most companies now have a website that contains more information than you would ever need. We show a brief extract of the detailed financial information on the website of Walmart.

Consolidated Financial Statements of Walmart Inc.

For the Fiscal Year Ended January 31, 2019

Table of Contents Page

One financial statement in the above list that we do not consider in this book is the Statement of Comprehensive Income. Comprehensive income can be considered to be the difference in the entity's total wealth at the beginning and at the end of the financial period. The owners' equity, that is, their "share" of the company, is the measure of wealth. A decline in equity indicates a decrease in wealth; an increase in equity indicates an increase in wealth. In making these calculations, it is assumed that there have been no direct transactions with shareholders, for example, the payments of dividends during the financial period.

The argument for the statement is that it provides more useful information than just profit because it shows all the gains and losses, both realized and unrealized, that increases or decreases the owners' equity, that is, wealth.

The International Accounting Standards Board introduced in 2009 a standard requiring a company to show a statement of comprehensive income in its annual report and accounts. The U.S. Statement of Financial Accounting Standards No. 130 (SFAS 130) requires the U.S. firms to report other comprehensive income. A U.S. study of the value relevance of the statement came to no firm conclusions but identified some issues concerning the use of the statement (Lin, Martinez, Wang, and Yang 2018).

A similar study was conducted by Mechelli and Cimini (2014) of the European countries where the international standard is followed. They concluded that despite the use of the same accounting standards, different motivations for various IFRS practices could lead to different accounting choices in countries. The information value of the comprehensive income statement was therefore questionable.

As the information value of the statement has been questioned, we will not discuss it further in this book. Obtaining financial information on large companies is not difficult. It is a matter of identifying the information you want and how you can best make judgments and conclusions. In the next section, we explain the three main financial statements that are key to conducting an analysis.

Three Main Financial Statements

In Chapter 1, we gave examples of financial reports from well-known companies. We also pointed out that these financial reports were contained in a document that could sometimes be over 300 pages in length. Now we are going to look at the three main financial statements contained in those lengthy reports that you will use to conduct a financial analysis. We introduced them in Chapter 1 but now we need to take a closer look.

The three statements give different but connected information. The Statement of Cash Flows tells you about cash movements and the Statement of Income gives information on profit. Both are concerned with events over a period of time. This may be one year or as little as three months. The statement of financial position is like a snapshot of the business at the end of the period. It tells you the amount of profit made and how it was generated. We explain in more detail below the contents of the three statements.

Statement of Cash Flow

This shows the movement of cash in and out of the organization over the financial period. It does **not** show profit. The statement records from where the entity received cash and how it has used it. The statement provides summative information on all inflows of cash received by a company from its ongoing operations as well as external investment sources. It also shows cash outflows for business activities as well as investments. Mostly, we need to identify the total cash coming into the organization and the total cost going out. There will be a difference between the two figures and this will be either a cash surplus or a cash deficit. If you are working in a small company, you will find the Bank's statement of interest.

Statement of Income

(Profit or Loss Statement)

This statement in the annual report may be named the statement of income or the profit or loss statement. In small businesses, they may refer to the Profit or Loss Account. Some companies issue a Statement of Comprehensive Income, which incorporates additional transactions and is not included in this analysis guide. The basic Statement of Income shows how well or poorly the entity has performed in conducting its business over a period of time to make a profit or suffer a loss. The statement does not show cash receipts and payments.

The main elements of the Statement will be the revenue that has been earned over that period of time and the expenses that have been incurred in generating that revenue. If the revenue exceeds the expenses, there will be a profit. In explaining our analysis later in this chapter, we usually take the profit before tax figure. The amount of tax you pay is decided by the tax authorities who have their own regulations and is not connected to our financial analysis. Remember that this Income Statement does not show cash movements. In other words, you can make a profit but still go bankrupt if people have not paid you for the goods and services you have delivered!

Statement of Financial Position

(Balance Sheet)

The Statement of Financial Position, also known as the balance sheet, is a financial snapshot of the business at a specific date and shows its financial position at the end of a period. The Statement of Financial Position will be dated on the very last day of that financial period. The main elements of the Statement of Financial Position are the assets that the company has, the investment by the shareholders and the liabilities of the company. As we explained in Chapter 1, the total of the assets held by the company will always match the total of liabilities.

You can consolidate your understanding of the basics of the three main financial statements by working through the following two simple examples. If you feel confident that you understand the statements, you can skip to the next section, which explains how to conduct a basic financial analysis.

Worked Examples

The following two examples are designed to demonstrate how the financial statements are drawn up to show the financial activities of a company. In real life, the financial statements of a large company may, at first, look very overwhelming but the same principles are followed as in the following example.

Example 1. Garden Statues

Jay Task decides to buy and sell garden statues. He starts the business with $500 of his own money. All his transactions are in cash. In January, he buys 20 statues for $100 each from his supplier, although by the end of the month he still owes the supplier for three statues. Of the 20 statues, he sells 17 of them at $150 each but has seven customers who have not yet paid for each of their statues.

To calculate the profit, we look at the transactions regardless of any cash paid or received. The results are shown on the following profit statement.

Jay Task Profit statement for the month of January	
Sales (17 statues at $150 each)	$2,550
Less costs of sales (17 statues at $100 each)	$1,700
Profit	$850

You can do a simple check on the above statement. On each statue, a profit of $50 was made. As 17 statues were sold with a profit of $50 on each statue, the total profit is $850. Jay may be pleased with this profit but how much cash does he have? He has sold 17 statues but has only received payment for 10 of them. He has paid his supplier for 17 statues at $100 each. We now need to draw up a cash statement to show these transactions.

Jay Task Cash statement for the month of January	
Investment by Jay	$500
Payment received (10 × $150)	$1,500
Total Cash in	$2,000
Payment to supplier (17 × $100)	$1700
Cash surplus	$300

Note that with both statements, and particularly with the cash statement, we are showing Jay as separate from his business. The two statements show us that Jay made a profit but, his business cannot afford to repay Jay for the $500 cash he invested.

If we want to understand Jay's business, we need both a profit statement and a cash statement. But even that does not tell us the complete story. We also need to know how Jay stands now and a balance sheet, also known as a statement of financial position, will give us the answer.

Below we have drawn up a two-sided balance sheet as this gives an immediate link to all the transactions. You will find that many companies present the balance sheet in a vertical format. It contains the same information as the horizontal format, which we show below.

Jay Task Balance sheet at the end of January			
Assets		Liabilities	
3 statues worth $100 each	$300	Owing to supplier (3 × $100)	$300
Customers owing (7 × $150)	$1050	Investment by owner	$500
Cash surplus	$300	Profit retained	$850
	$1650		$1650

You will notice that the balance sheet differs from the other two statements. The balance sheet is a snapshot at the end of January. The other two statements showed events for the entire month.

These three statements give a good overview of the company. It made a profit of $850, which was good, but the cash position was less favorable. The company cannot afford to pay Jay the full profit it made in the period. It cannot repay him the investment he made and can just pay the suppliers.

Jay can take action to improve the situation but he needs the three separate statements to obtain a full picture. By drawing up the three separate financial statements, we have a better understanding of how the company is performing. To improve our investigations, it would be helpful to have the results for several financial periods. We can then analyze where there are financial problems that require attention.

The above simple example explains the foundations but the full financial statements are more complex and incorporate much more information. If we are going to assess these larger companies, we need a system for doing it methodically. The best procedure is to use analytical techniques, and in this chapter and in Chapter 3, we explain how you can conduct your own financial ratio analysis.

If you have no prior knowledge of accounting, it can be difficult to understand how the above three financial statements interact and the value of calculating ratios. In this section, we give an example of a startup business to reinforce your knowledge of the main financial statements and to demonstrate what they tell us about the operation of a business.

Example 2. Happy Parties

Megan Tont decides on January 1, 2020 to start a business organizing children's birthday parties. She uses the name *Happy Parties* for the business. For every party booked, she requires a deposit of $50 when the booking is made and a final payment of $200 within 7 days of the party being held. The costs to her for booking the room, supplying food, and drink are $150 per party.

In the first three months, she holds 10 parties. Two of the clients still need to pay their balances of $200 each and she owes $150 to the supplier for room, food, and drinks.

The critical point to remember is that the financial statements we construct are for Happy Parties and not for Megan Tont. We will start with the cash statements. Remember this is a record of cash coming in and going out of the business.

Cash statement for Happy Parties for the three months to March 31, 2020	
Receipts	$
Booking deposits (10 parties by $50)	500
Final receipts (8 × $200)	1,600
Total of cash in	2,100
Payments	
9 parties by $150 (one payment owing by Megan)	1,350
Positive cash balance	750

Megan has been fortunate in her choice of business as it is what is known as a "cash up front" business. In other words, Megan did not have to immediately use her own money but relied on receiving the cash from her customers before the business had to settle its own debts. As far as receipts are concerned, $400 is still owed, this being the final payments for two parties.

The business also had advertising costs of $100, which have not yet been paid. It also owes the $150 booking fee. The positive cash balance is correct but only gives part of the financial story. In this example, and in real life, cash and the actual profit made are usually different amounts. This would not apply to a "cash only" business but we are not concerned with those.

If we want to know the profit figure for Happy Parties, we need to draw up a profit or loss account, also known as an Income Statement.

Income statement for Happy Parties for the three months to March 31, 2020		
Sales from holding 10 parties ($250 × 10)		$2,500
Costs of holding 10 parties ($150 × 10)		$1,500
Advertising costs	$100	$1,600
Profit		$900

We have two apparently different results about the same activity, the parties, but we are looking at two separate financial statements designed to provide us with different information on which we may take action. The cash statement tells us about the movements of cash. The Income Statement or profit or loss statement tells us the results of transactions entered into regardless of any payments made or not made.

We now look at the third statement for Happy Parties—the Balance Sheet. This will provide a "snapshot" of the business at a particular date. For some companies, this will be at the end of their financial years, although many report quarterly or half-yearly. However, the information provided will be the assets the company has. This will be for such items as land, buildings, machinery, and vehicles. There may also be people who owe money to the business and these are known as debtors.

In addition to assets, the balance sheet shows the liabilities of the company. Happy Parties owes for the advertising and for one party that has been held. If we draw up the balance sheet correctly, the total of the assets equals the total of the liabilities. Remember we are looking at the business and we consider Megan to be separate from it.

Balance sheet for Happy Parties as on March 31, 2020			
	Assets		*Liabilities*
(Debtors) payments due from clients	$400	*Creditors*	
		Booking fee	$150
Cash in hand	$750	Advertising costs	$100
		Profit	$900
	$1,150		$1,150

The people who owe us money are known as debtors and that is an asset, as long as they pay us! The people to whom we owe money are known as creditors and that is a liability. And of course, the balance sheet does balance with assets having the same total as liabilities.

The profit of $900 belongs to the owner of the business and Megan may want it. Unfortunately, the business only has $750 in cash. If it pays this to Megan then the cash in hand will not appear on the balance sheet. Also, the amount of profit kept in the business will be reduced by that amount to $150 and the balance sheet still balances.

The above example is a simplification and with major companies, you will find many more entries. One of the major factors with most businesses is that they need cash to operate. With small businesses, it may be possible to arrange a loan but this will mean that interest has to be paid and the full amount of the loan has to be repaid at some time.

The examples we give above may appear too easy, but the procedure is somewhat similar for large companies. Below we show a simplified extract of the Consolidated Statement of Income from the FORM 10-K of Walt Disney for the Fiscal Year Ended September 29, 2018.

CONSOLIDATED STATEMENTS OF INCOME 2018 in $ Millions	
Total revenues	59,434
Costs and expenses:	
Cost of services (exclusive of depreciation and amortization)	(27,528)
Cost of products (exclusive of depreciation and amortization)	(5,198)
Selling, general, administrative and other	(8,860)
Depreciation and amortization	(3,011)
Total costs and expenses	(44,597)
Net income	13,066

We emphasize that this is only a small extract from a very lengthy document. You can easily download the full document and much more information from their website at

https://thewaltdisneycompany.com/investor-relations/#reports

The point to note is that the above statement does not tell us about cash movements. Neither does it tell us about the company's financial position at the end of the period. That information is to be found in the balance sheet (statement of financial position).

Another way to obtain funding is to seek investors. This can be done by an issue of shares in the company. The amount that is invested is usually referred to as "capital" or "equity." Bear in mind that the capital amount shown on the balance sheet is the amount originally invested by shareholders plus any profits that have been made but not yet paid to them in the form of dividends.

The other important factor to note is that share prices for a company on a stock exchange do not usually match the capital or equity figure shown on the balance sheet of a company. The current share price represents the amount somebody is willing to pay the owner of the shares to obtain their interest in a company. In making this decision, they will refer to the financial statements but also make judgments on competitors, the nature of the industry, and the movements in the share market. In Chapter 3, we explain the ratios that investors use in making decisions.

We show below only a few main items from the balance sheet of the Ford Motor Company. The balance sheet balances but there will be some items in there that may cause confusion, which we will resolve in the subsequent chapters.

FORD MOTOR COMPANY AND SUBSIDIARIES CONSOLIDATED BALANCE SHEET (in millions) December 31, 2018	
ASSETS	
Total assets	$ 256,540
LIABILITIES	
Total liabilities	$220,474
Redeemable non-controlling interest	$100
EQUITY	
Total equity	$35,966
Total liabilities and equity	$256,540

We emphasize that above we have extracted only the main totals from the original document. There are over 25 separate items on the balance sheet and the amounts for the previous year (2017) are also given. The individual items are explained by the accompanying notes that also cover many pages. For our purposes and the analysis, we explain in subsequent chapters, only the main items that are important. The full information can be found on

https://corporate.ford.com › microsites › assets › files › sr18-form-10-k

The above example demonstrates that the balance sheet does balance but it introduces a subject that we have not yet discussed—equity. As we explained above, companies have shareholders who own the company. Directors do not "own" the business as such but are responsible for running the business for the benefit of shareholders. It is possible that they also own shares.

Equity is ownership of assets that may have debts or other liabilities attached to them. Beware! As we explained above, the value of equity shown on a company's balance sheet is not directly related to the share price that you see on the Stock Exchange daily. It is the performance of a company that affects the share price.

At this stage, you should have an understanding of the purposes and information values of the three main financial statements. We are now going to demonstrate how you can use your knowledge to conduct an analysis of the financial position and performance of a company.

Basic Analysis

The first step in an analysis is to carry out an initial review. This can be conducted very easily and gives you some understanding of the business in which you are interested. The following three approaches are simple and quick to apply.

1. Trend analysis, which looks at changes over a period of time and puts hard numbers on them. The period may be as simple as comparing this year with last year or includes several years. Usually, two main items are selected to do the analysis and sales and profit are frequently the most interesting ones.
2. Vertical analysis is where you may only take one component, such as sales or profit, but conduct an analysis over several years. This will signal whether activity is steadily increasing or decreasing over a period of time.
3. Comparative analysis, which is simply comparing the results of one company with another over a period of years. If available, you can make the comparison with the industry average where this information is available. This can be linked to a trend or vertical analysis. Clearly, it is best to compare companies that are in the same industry or related industries.

Trend Analysis

The purpose of this analysis is to find out whether the amount shown on the financial statements for the present financial period is better or worse than in the previous financial periods. We are examining data for particular financial activities or results either by a simple comparison with the previous year or over an extended period. This could be years, months, or even weeks if the data is available. Needless to say, the results most of us are interested in are sales, usually referred to as revenue, and profits.

In the following simple example, we compare the present year with the previous year for both revenue (sales) and profit. There are sometimes several types of profits referred to on the Income Statement, which we explain later in this chapter. The comparison is the current year to the previous year. We show that the change is in dollars and percentages.

Year to year analysis				
	Current year	Previous year	Change	% Change
Sales	$3,000	$2,600	$400	15%
Profits	$460	$420	$40	10%

The above is a simple analysis where we are comparing only two years. We have taken the dollar amount of change and divided it by the previous year's amounts of sales and profit to give the percentage change. We have calculated only the main amounts and not calculated the percentage points as the differences are insignificant. If you can only find differences by working to the percentage point, you may wish to consider whether the difference is only a slight sneeze and not a terminal disease.

The obvious question we need to answer is the reason why revenue increased by an appreciable percentage but profit did not. If we analyze the results of a real company, we would usually find that the directors provide an explanation for this anomaly in their annual report and accounts. Some examples of these are given later in the chapter.

One possible reason we can suggest for the trends is that costs have increased but it was not possible to increase the selling prices of the products. Another reason may be that the company has purposely decreased the selling price of their products to enter into new markets. If the data you have is analyzed for a company you own or you are an employee, it should be possible to ascertain the reason.

A comparison of this year's data with the previous year can be revealing, but it is much more useful if you can compare the data for at least five years or possibly more. In the following example, we have the amounts for five years for the revenue and the total costs. Most companies have on their websites the annual report and accounts for many years, so obtaining the data should not cause a problem. You should be aware that accounting regulations are amended from time to time. This includes both International Financial Reporting Standards and the U.S. regulations.

If you are conducting an analysis of organizational performance over several years, you should check if there have been any changes in the financial regulations. This includes charities and other types of organizations. An example of a substantial change is the issue by the FASB in 2016 of *Not-for-Profit Entities (Topic 958)*. There was a diversity of reporting practices around contributions, and it is considered that the Update was added to give clarity to and strengthen not-for-profit financial reporting (Fitzsimons, McCarthy, and Silliman 2018).

In the following example, we show the revenue and total costs of a fictitious company over a five-year period.

Trend analysis of revenue and costs in $000 for five years					
	2014	2015	2016	2017	2018
Revenue	110	112	114	113	112
Total costs	80	85	87	87	88

We could now calculate the percentage changes but even the basic figures show significant differences that require further investigation. Over the five-year period, revenue peaked in 2016 but has declined again. Over that period, costs have gradually increased. Further investigation would be required to find out the reasons. One may be that the market has tightened so that the company has had to reduce its selling price per item. However, the costs of production may have increased for other reasons but cannot be passed on to customers. In the annual report, the Directors usually explain changes in the economic environment that have impacted their activities.

Some managers find that a line graph of the trend pinned on their office notice board is a helpful tool for focusing attention when it is needed. If the data is available on a weekly or monthly basis, the graph visually demonstrates possible problems and assists you as a manager making financial decisions.

Same Size or Vertical Analysis

This analysis is usually conducted by calculating all the costs over several years and calculating them as a percentage of the sales figure. You may find that a company has already provided this information in its annual report. The following example uses the profit and loss account to demonstrate the calculations for one year.

	Vertical analysis for one year			
	2019		2018	
	$000	%	$000	%
Sales	200		250	
Materials	80	40.0	110	44.0
Wages	50	25.0	70	28.0
Overheads	25	12.5	25	10.0
Transport costs	15	7.5	20	8.0
Depreciation	5	2.5	5	2.0
Profit	25	12.5	20	8.0

It is impossible to draw any firm conclusions from the above analysis but it does focus the investigations one can usefully make. Usually, with such a substantial drop in sales over one period, you would anticipate the profit is also dropping, but in this example, it has increased in absolute terms. A closer examination shows that materials and wages have both decreased in absolute terms.

With a decrease in sales, one would anticipate this but the decrease in percentage terms is higher than one would expect. This requires closer investigation. Overhead and depreciation costs have remained the same in absolute terms. As these are usually fixed in nature, regardless of changes in activity, it is not surprising that the percentage figures have increased in 2019.

The first step therefore is to determine the reason for the decline in the sales figure. Is the same volume being sold and the company has reduced its selling price or has there been a decrease in the volume sold? At this stage of the investigation, we would favor the former but further analysis is required.

Comparative Analysis

You can easily conduct a trend or vertical analysis for one company and draw conclusions. However, the knowledge you can gain from analyzing one company can be greatly improved with comparators. This can be a comparison with one or more companies, or comparisons with industry averages. You can do the calculations yourself but the website provides substantial amount of information.

You will find it is best, at least as a starter, to concentrate on companies in the same industry. Different industries have different profiles. For example, a car manufacturer will have very different revenues and costs than a chain of hotels. If you search the web, you will find that there are numerous sources of the ratios for specific industries. These averages are extremely helpful as they provide a guide to competitor's performance. Compare their own data figure with those averages, and it will help you to draw conclusions. You will find that a visit to the website will provide numerous guides to industry averages.

Errors and Frauds

In conducting an analysis of an organization's financial statements, some degree of caution should be exercised. Capturing all the activities of the organization in financial terms and explaining them in a structured manner is a difficult task. There is always the possibility of errors occurring and, in some cases, fraud.

Estimates

Imagine you have a worker who is paid $20 per hour. At the end of the month, you look at his time sheet and it states 100 hours worked.

You therefore show in your financial accounts the cost of wages as $2,000. However, suppose the worker made an honest error in its recording and he worked more or less hours. Your financial statements are incorrect.

You need to pay for the electricity for the period but the invoice has not yet arrived despite requests you have made. You make your best estimate but it may be somewhat later before you know the actual amount. Another possible example is where a customer is refusing to pay the full amount for the service she has received and wants a $500 discount. The matter is unresolved. What do you put in your financial statements at the end of the financial period?

Accountants have to make the best estimates in these circumstances and are guided by the requirements of financial accounting standards. This does mean that the financial statements that you examine may not have the 100 percent accuracy that you believe. In taking a company's activities and describing them in financial terms has difficulties and errors may occur.

An investigation (Alali and Wang 2017) of corporate reporting quality from 2000–2014 concluded that "regulation and enforcement may play an important role in deterring, preventing, and detecting financial manipulation, but the level of discretion applied and the resources available to regulators limit the effectiveness of such regulations." A comprehensive study of the literature on financial reporting misconduct from the perspectives of law, accounting, and finance noted that many of the most infamous cases of corporate misconduct involve accounting misrepresentations, with Enron and WorldCom being two classic examples (Amiram et al. 2017).

Information Quality

Your analysis will depend on the quality and accuracy of the financial statements. You must check that the financial statements have been properly audited and there should be confirmation by independent auditors of this accompanying the statements. Even this is not always a guarantee on the quality of the statements. Although accounting standards set out the procedures for accounting transactions and the information to be disclosed, there can be errors and sometimes deliberate misinformation.

One study (Johnston and Pittachi 2017) examined the comment letters the Securities and Exchange Commission (SEC) sends to companies where there are questions regarding the documents it has submitted. The research discovered that nearly half of all the comments involve accounting application, financial reporting, and disclosure issues. More than 17 percent of the sample cases result in immediate amended filings to resolve the issues arising from the comment letters, and financial statements and/ or footnotes are frequently revised.

One type of fraud that is extremely difficult to identify is that by an outside entity against an organization, sometimes with the collusion of that organization. Carmichael (2020) points out that these minor collusions by an organization with outside parties does not usually impact the financial statements, although there are financial benefits to those perpetrating them. However, he argues and gives examples of major frauds that third or external parties have perpetrated that have materially misstated the financial statements.

One should not conclude from these studies that most companies' financial statements are questionable. We do not wish to overemphasize the possibility of error or fraud. The major frauds that have been discovered over the years hit the headlines but undiscovered errors or fraud can be present. Our advice is if the types of analysis we explain in the next chapter give results that do not seem credible, you check your calculations carefully and with any decisions you are making, you proceed with caution.

Conclusions

The first look at a complete annual report and accounts issued by a company can be very intimidating. This can be true of large companies and even small businesses. The approach we recommend in this chapter is to keep focused on the three key financial statements and the purpose of these statements.

The Income Statement or Profit or Loss Statement tells you about profit for a financial period, the Statement of cash flows reveals the cash coming in and out during the financial period and the Statement of

Financial Position or Balance Sheet shows the assets and liabilities of the company at the end of the financial period.

You will find that either in their annual report, or on their website, companies provide a considerable amount of information on how they performed during the financial period. Also, on their printed document or on their website, they will comment on their results. In this chapter, we have shown how you can conduct an initial investigation by using a trend analysis, vertical analysis, and comparative analysis.

Although an organization may not be large enough or legally required to publish a complete annual report, you will find that the smallest organization, including your own, usually will prepare the three financial statements we have discussed in this chapter.

In the next chapter, we will explain how you can conduct a thorough examination of the financial performance of a company by conducting a profitability analysis, a liquidity analysis, and a cash analysis.

Action Plan

All companies generate substantial amounts of financial information. With larger companies, this may be publicly available and you should visit the company's website. There are three key financial statements that we have described in this chapter. If you know the reasons you want the information, the choices are:

1. Statement of Income (Profit or Loss statement). This will show you the revenue that the company has earned and the costs that have been incurred to arrive at the amount of profit, or in bad times, the amount of the loss.
2. Statement of Cash Flow, which records the movements of cash in and out of the business. We have explained in this chapter how profit and cash are different. We would emphasize that a company may make a profit but still have problems with its management of cash flows.
3. Statement of Financial Position (Balance Sheet). This is like a financial snapshot of the business at one point in time. It shows all the assets that the company has and all its liabilities.

If you followed our advice in Chapter 1 and decided upon the reason you wanted the information, you can focus on the particular financial statement of interest to you. If you want a general picture, you may want to examine all the three financial statements. Remember that if you are only looking at one year, there may be factors of which you are unaware, that means it is not representative. Our advice is to conduct a trend analysis as we have explained in this chapter. In the next chapter, we demonstrate how you can conduct a sophisticated analysis of these three main financial statements.

CHAPTER 3

Financial Statement Analysis

About This chapter

To conduct any analysis of a company's financial statements, you need to have a basic understanding of the information it is giving. The names of the financial statements demonstrate their purpose and we explained these in Chapter 2. At this stage, we are going to expand on our explanations before demonstrating how to analyze the information.

In the first part of this chapter, we give extracts from three major companies in three different countries. We have selected only those items that we consider important for our analysis but we provide the website link if you wish to make a fuller examination. As you become more experienced, you will be able to conduct more sophisticated analysis. At this stage, we are demonstrating that you can look at a seemingly complex financial statement and extract the figures you require to conduct your own analysis that meets your reasons for your interest, as stated at the end of Chapter 1.

In the second part of this chapter, we explain how to conduct a sophisticated analysis of an organization's financial statements. We focus on analyzing the profitability, liquidity, and efficiency of the company and also on the control of cash.

Company Examples

Before we look at conducting our own analysis, it is useful to see how major companies report financial information and comment on it. You will find that their annual reports contain substantial explanations and analysis from its own Directors and these comments can be well in excess of 100 pages. You can obtain a printed copy of the report but you will find that most companies have a website, which contains an abundance of information. We are concentrating specifically on the extracts we have taken for three different companies and three different financial statements. There are sometimes differences in terminology so we have included other wording you may encounter.

Example 1

Profit or Loss Statement,
Statement of Comprehensive income,
Statement of Financial Performance.

Depending on the type of organization and the regulations it is following, the title of the statement can vary, but you are interested in the statement that will show sales (sometimes referred to as *turnover* or *revenue*), its main costs and the profit or loss it has made in that financial period. The important concept to keep in mind is that this statement does not give you any information on cash.

We have extracted below the main figures from Unilever, which is a UK company following International Financial Reporting Standards that require not only a Statement of Income but also a Statement of Comprehensive Income. As explained in Chapter 2, we are excluding the Statement of Comprehensive Income from our discussions as it includes some complexities, which are not relevant to the analysis we demonstrate in this chapter.

For our present analysis, we are only interested in the "Consolidated Income Statement" and we have extracted the amounts for "Turnover," which is the equivalent of a "Sales" figure and the amount of Net Profit. We would advise you to carry out any profit analysis with the amount of profit prior to the amount of taxation the company must pay. Taxation rates are decided by the government of the country and not by the company. The full financial statements in our Unilever example can be found on:

https://unilever.com › Images › unilever-annual-report-and-accounts-2...

Unilever plc (Extract) CONSOLIDATED INCOME STATEMENT for the year ended 31 December		
	2019–2018	
	€ million	€ million
Turnover	51,980	50,982
Profit before taxation	8,289	12,360

The company addresses these results on page 6 of its annual report where Alan Jope, Chief Executive Officer states:

> In markets as dynamic and fast-moving as ours, speed is essential, both in seizing opportunities to meet changing consumer preferences but also in responding when our business is under competitive challenge. While we do this well on many occasions and in many parts of the world, we haven't yet developed the consistency of response that I am looking for everywhere and this was apparent in 2019. We made some important organisational changes during the year—including flattening our market structure under a newly created Chief Operating Officer position—which I am confident will help to make Unilever a faster and even more operationally effective business.

This is a small extract from a report of 183 pages. With the results for only two years, it would be unwise to draw any firm conclusions. However, even if you have not understood financial statements before, you can see that given the profit or loss for several years, you could conduct a trend analysis as shown in the previous chapter. This would enable you to assess the company's progress over several years.

Example 2

Balance Sheet

Statement of Financial Position

This statement provides information on the financial status of the organization at one point in time, usually the end of the financial year. It will show the detail of what the company owns, such as land and buildings, materials, money it is owed, and any cash it has. These are its assets. These are balanced by its liabilities such as the investment by shareholders, loans from the banks, and any debts it owes. The following example is from the Australian company Coles Group. We have extracted only the main data. It is noticeable that this company calculates the percentage change for the year. The full reports can be seen on:

https://colesgroup.com.au › investors › page=results-and-reports

Balance sheet The balance sheet statements for the Group in $ MILLION			
	30 JUNE 2019	30 JUNE 2018	CHANGE
Total assets	9,777.0	12,544.7	(22.1%)
Total liabilities	6,419.9	9,295.1	(30.9%)
Net assets	3,357.1	3249.6	

This small extract is from a report of 107 pages. From this extract, it is evident that the total assets and liabilities have reduced considerably. The reason for this is given in page 23 of their report, which states:

The reduction in inventories, property, plant and equipment, deferred tax assets and intangible assets is largely the result of the transfer of Kmart, Target and Officeworks (KTO) to Wesfarmers as part of the corporate restructure associated with the demerger.

Example 3

Cash Flow Statement

This statement is all about cash. It shows the financial funds coming into the company, such as cash, cheques, interest, and the financial funds going out. If more money comes in than goes out, that is usually good news. If more goes out than comes in, there may be problems that require investigation. Below we have extracted the amounts from the financial report from Apple. The company gave the figures for three years, but we have shown only the two years 2018 and 2017.

Apple Inc. https://investor.apple.com › investor-relations

CONSOLIDATED STATEMENTS OF CASH FLOWS (In millions)		
Years ended	September 29, 2018	September 30, 2017
Cash and cash equivalents, beginning of the year	$ 20,289	$ 20,484
Cash generated by/(used in) investing activities	16,066	(46,446)
Cash used in financing activities	(87,876)	(17,974)
Increase/(Decrease) in cash and cash equivalents	5,624	(195)
Cash and cash equivalents, end of the year	$ 25,913	$ 20,289

The statement of cash flows is regarded as an important source of information to understand the management of the company and as an alarm if there are problems. We will explain later in this chapter how the cash flow statement can be a crucial input into analyzing a company and gaining an understanding of its possible progress in the future.

On the Apple website, there are comments from the Directors on the financial results for its fiscal 2020 first quarter ended December 28, 2019. As far as the cash position is concerned, Luca Maestri, Apple's CFO reported that the very strong business performance drove an all-time net income record of $22.2 billion and generated operating cash flow of $30.5 billion, and added that Apple maintains their target of reaching a net cash neutral position over time.

Conducting an Analysis

Having explained the purpose of the three main financial statements, we can now consider how to analyze the results. This can allow us to examine an organization's financial activities over a period of time or to compare it with other organizations.

Ratios are usually based on a company's financial statements but an analysis is not only about the calculation of the ratios. You can use a simple spreadsheet model on your computer to calculate hundreds of ratios. The value of ratios is selecting the ones that address the aspect of the company in which you are most interested and then analyzing the results and drawing conclusions. Experience will help you produce a more sophisticated analysis and also comments made by the company and by financial analysts can confirm or challenge your own interpretations.

If you are making comparisons with two or more companies, you must ensure that the data is prepared on a comparable basis. The presence of International Financial Reporting Standards has greatly improved comparability with certain countries but there are items where alternative accounting treatments may be used. This is particularly relevant if you are comparing a U.S. company to a foreign company. As explained previously, the Financial Accounting Standards Board in the United States regulates financial accounting in that country.

Also keep in mind, when conducting an analysis with companies in other countries that, although the accounting regulations may be comparable, there may be national differences in actual business practices. A study in three countries found that the U.S. manufacturing corporations have higher liquidity levels compared with German and Japanese manufacturing corporations. German manufacturing corporations have higher liability levels compared with the U.S. and Japanese manufacturing corporations. The average collection period of accounts receivable and the average payment period of accounts payable are significantly shorter in the United States (Meric, Gunder, Chung, and Meric 2019).

Numerous ratios can be calculated. We have selected the most common ones and grouped them into profitability ratios, liquidity and efficiency ratios, and cash ratios. There are no set definitions of these ratios. Different terms are used to identify them and the data for calculating the ratio may be different. You should always check when you are making comparisons that you are using the same terms and definitions.

One word of caution before we explain the ratios. Do not obtain the financial statements of a company and try to immediately calculate every ratio we describe below. You will find it more enlightening if you are very clear on what you wish to analyze and the reason.

You may be interested on whether the company compares well with other companies, or with previous year's performance as far as generating profit. Then calculate and explore the profitability ratios. If you are interested in the financial strengths and weaknesses of a company, you are advised to examine its liquidity and efficiency ratios. If you are worried that the company may go bankrupt, then calculate the cash ratios. As you become more experienced, you will be able to select the ratios that you require to conduct a full analysis.

Profitability Analysis

Profit is calculated by identifying the costs incurred by an entity during the financial period and deducting this amount from the revenue for that period. Profit is therefore a balancing figure. If the costs are higher than the revenue for the same period, there will be a loss. You should note that we invariably use the figure for profit before tax. In all countries, the tax authorities have their own rules and regulations. They apply these to calculate the amount of taxable profit the company has made. This may have little connection with the profit the company has calculated using accounting, and not tax, regulations.

People buying shares or lending money to a company do so in anticipation that the company is making, and will continue to make, profits. One can also argue that if you are going to work for a company, you want it to be profitable. If you are in a business that supplies goods or services to a company, you want it to be successful so that you can stay in business.

The profitability ratios concentrate on financial performance. The four ratios we explain are:

- Return on capital employed - ROCE (also known as return on net assets employed RONA)
- Net asset turnover (also known as capital turnover)
- Net profit margin (also known as Return on Sales - ROS)
- Gross profit margin

There are no standard definitions for the above terms, so we use the following explanations that are commonly applied.

Return on Capital Employed (ROCE)

The "return" term usually means profit before interest and tax (PBIT). You will find this figure on the Income Statement of a company. Larger companies may identify this as operating profit or earnings before interest and tax (EBIT). Smaller companies may use the terms net profit or net earnings.

The capital employed is the investment made in the business and this is usually identified as the total invested by shareholders. One method of calculation, which usually should give the same answer, is to deduct the current liabilities from the total assets. You should be able to identify these figures on the balance sheet.

The ROCE measures the percentage return on the total investment of funds in the business. This demonstrates management's effectiveness in the amount of profit they can generate on the funds over which they have control.

$$\text{ROCE} = \frac{\text{Profit before interest and tax}}{\text{Capital employed}} \times 100$$

ROCE should reflect the element of risk in the investment and can be compared with interest rates for other investments where there is a very small risk of losing your money.

Net Asset Turnover (Capital Turnover)

This ratio measures the number of times the net assets have been used (i.e., turned over) during the year to achieve the sales revenue. Generally, the more frequently the net assets are "turned over," the more success-ful is the business. The ratio shows the number of times that the capital employed has been used during the year to achieve the sales revenue, which we refer to as turnover. It is usually expressed as the number of times rather than a percentage and the formula is:

$$\frac{\text{Turnover}}{\text{Capital employed}}$$

The Net Profit Margin

PBIT (Profit Before Interest and Tax) Margin

This ratio measures the percentage return on sales. The formula is:

$$\frac{\text{Profit before interest and tax}}{\text{Turnover}} \times 100$$

This is the profit before interest and tax expressed as a percentage of the sales figure. It shows the percentage profit a company makes on sales after deducting all the expenses but before interest charges and tax.

Gross Profit Margin

This measures gross profit as a percentage of sales and is a good indicator of how successful the business is in its basic trading operations. For managers and investors, this is a significant ratio in assessing business performance. The gross profit margin measures the gross profit as a percentage of sales. The formula is:

$$\frac{\text{Gross profit}}{\text{Turnover}} \times 100$$

Worked Example – Profitability Analysis

It is helpful to see how we construct these ratios and interpret the findings. The following example is a comparison between two small companies at one date. If you do not have two or more companies for comparison, you can analyze only one company using the same ratios over a period of time to ascertain whether there have been changes. In our following fictitious example of comparisons, we have named the two companies as Focus and Hilight.

Both companies supply electrical equipment. We demonstrate the calculation of the ratios and their interpretation. In this example, we concentrate on the ratios that are based on the data in the Balance Sheet and Income Statement to conduct a profitability analysis. The procedure and explanation we have given can also be used for a large company listed on a stock exchange.

There are two companies operating in the same industry. The data from the Income Statement that we have for 2020 is:

	Focus	Hilight
	$000	$000
Sales	120	240
Gross profit	60	90
Net profit	20	25

The above figures illustrate that measured by the sales and profit amounts, Hilight is the bigger of the two companies and has made both the largest gross profit and net profit. But the question we wish to answer is which is the most *profitable* company. We can analyze the above financial information by calculating the two profitability ratios that are based on the information in the Income Statement:

	Focus	Hilight
	000	000
Gross profit margin	$60 × 100 = 50%	$130 × 100 = 54.2%
	$120	$240
Net profit margin	$20 × 100 = 16.7%	$35 × 100 = 14.6%
	$120	$240

The above figures show that, although Hilight has the largest gross profit and net profit in absolute terms, our opinion on the most profitable company changes when we calculate the ratios. Hilight's gross profit in absolute terms is over double that of Focus and the gross margin ratio is 4.2 percent higher. The assumption is that Hilight is a much bigger company and its selling prices may be slightly higher or it can charge more for its goods. The gross profit margin is essentially the difference between the price it pays for materials and goods and the price it can sell them at.

When we calculate the net profit margin, the margin for Hilight is 14.6 percent, which is lower than that for Focus, which is 16.7 percent. Our conclusion could be that Hilight is a more expensive company to operate. Possibly, it spends more on advertising, wages, administration, and other operational costs than Focus.

We need more financial information to pursue our investigations, but this simple example demonstrates that taking the absolute figures for gross profit and net profit show that Hilight is a bigger company but the ratios indicate that Focus would appear to have greater control of its operating costs. Our analysis and interpretation would be improved if we had the data for several years and could therefore conduct a comparative trend analysis as explained in Chapter 2.

Liquidity and Efficiency Analysis

A scrutiny of a company's profits is important but it is essential to know how rich or poor it is. A poor company could become bankrupt! Even a company that appears to be successful in making profits can have financial difficulties. You may have conducted your profitability analysis and be satisfied with the financial performance of the company but you need to go further.

There is the important question on whether the company can manage its cash. Remember that profit and cash are different measures. A company can appear very profitable but may go bankrupt because of poor cash management. We need to look in detail at how a company manages its cash position. We list below the ratios that help you determine whether it is managed efficiently.

- Working capital ratio
- Current test

- Inventory (stock) turnover
- Debtor collection period
- Creditor payment period

We demonstrate the method for calculating these ratios in the following examples. None of the calculations are complicated but you do need comparisons, either over a period of time or with other companies. This enables you to judge whether the company you are investigating is improving or not. Without comparisons, you are unable to draw any conclusions. Useful information can be obtained from the following sources

- The financial statements for the same company for previous years.
- The financial statements of similar companies
- Industry ratios
- Comments in the financial press
- The website of the company, if there is one

Working Capital Ratio

This is a ratio that captures both liquidity and efficiency. Working capital is calculated by deducting current liabilities from current assets. The equation is:

$$\text{Working capital} = \text{Current Assets} - \text{Current Liabilities}$$

A company must be alert to the amount of investment made in non-current assets, such as buildings and machinery. It needs to be even more alert regarding the money it is using in its daily operations. This is known as the investment in working capital. Insufficient working capital can cause a company to become bankrupt. The use of ratios assists a company to manage its working capital. It also reveals the immediate financial health of the company to the investors. The following ratios explore the different aspects of liquidity.

Current Test

This is a liquidity ratio that shows the relationship between the business's liquid (current) assets and its current liabilities. In other words, it shows whether the company looks able to pay its current debts without seeking loans. Inventory (stock) is a current asset but it has to be sold before you can turn it into cash. It is therefore normal practice to use current assets minus the value of stock when calculating the current test. Similarly, we normally only take the creditors that have to be paid within the next 12 months, as this is our present concern. If we have creditors we have to pay after 12 months, this is a separate and less urgent consideration. The calculation is:

$$\frac{\text{Current assets} - \text{inventory}}{\text{Creditors: amounts due within one year}}$$

As you can see from the equation above, all the figures you want should be found on the balance sheet. The calculation can either show the percentages or the times figure. You need to remember that the accounts are prepared on a prudent basis and that the amounts owed to current creditors at the end of the financial year will be due at different times in the next financial year. However, most analysts would agree that the ratio should not fall below 1:1. If it does, it means that the company owes more money to its current creditors than it can collect from its current debtors.

It is difficult to generalize on what the levels of liquidity should be. However, if you do the analysis for several years and the ratio is declining, the obvious worry is whether the company will be able to continue to pay its debts.

Inventory (Stock) Turnover

This is an efficiency ratio that measures the average number of times the stock has been sold and replaced during the year. There is the reasonable assumption that quick stock turnover is the mark of an efficient company. The turnover rate will depend on the type of product and the nature of the industry. What one does not want to see is the factory pressing on with production if the sales team cannot find customers. The formula for the ratio is:

$$\frac{\text{Cost of sales}}{\text{Average inventory}}$$

You need to look at the profit and loss account to obtain the figures for the average inventory. If they are disclosed, you can use the following formula:

$$\frac{\text{Opening inventory + Closing inventory}}{2}$$

However, if a figure for opening stock is not provided, you can use closing stock for the previous year as the proxy.

Debtor Collection Period

This is an efficiency ratio that gives an indication of the effectiveness of the management of working capital. It measures the average time trade debtors (customers) have taken to pay the business for goods and services bought on credit over the year. The debtor collection period in days is calculated using the following formula:

$$\frac{\text{Trade debtors}}{\text{Turnover}} \times 365$$

If a breakdown of debtors is not given in the balance sheet, it is likely that the figure for trade debtors is given in the notes to the accounts.

Creditor Payment Period

This is an efficiency ratio that measures the average time that the business has taken to pay its trade creditors. The creditor payment period in days is calculated using the following formula:

$$\frac{\text{Trade creditors}}{\text{Purchases}} \times 365$$

Although some people do not like debts and prefer to pay invoices and statements as soon as they receive them rather than wait until they are due, this is not always a good way of managing cash. Receiving goods on credit is the equivalent of having an interest-free loan. If the supplier does not give credit, the business may have to go into overdraft to pay cash for the goods. This does not mean that a business should wait until it receives a solicitor's letter or risk supplies being cut off, but from a financial point of view, management should take the maximum time allowed to pay trade creditors, whilst at the same time, collect payment from trade debtors as quickly as possible.

The premise underpinning these ratios is that companies should be able to pay their current liabilities from their current assets. If they are unable to do this, they must seek more finance. This can be difficult if the economy is in decline or its future strength uncertain. However, not all countries may have the same approach. A study of industries found that Canadian firms invest less in working capital than their U.S. counterparts (Khokhar 2019).

Cash Analysis

A thorough analysis of the management of working capital is essential. One important aspect is cash. It is so important that companies publish a Cash Statement. It is essential that a business has control of its cash flows, and in this section, we describe the main ratios used to assess cash flows, both in and out of the company. The main ratios are:

- Cash flows from operating activities
- Cash recovery rate
- Cash flow per share
- Free cash flow ratio

Before we focus on these ratios, a word of caution. For individuals, identifying cash or the lack of it, is a relatively easy task. With organizations, it becomes more complex and the Financial Accounting Standards

Board has issued guidance. In 1979, FASB required the statement of cash flows as a required financial statement. Practitioners and preparers have had difficulty in implementing or applying the standard. The FASB has issued guidance, but it is argued that several issues are still unresolved and significant changes may still take place (Schutte and Duncan 2019).

Cash Flow from Operations

With any business, it is critical to determine whether it has sufficient cash to pay its current liabilities—its current debts. If not, the result could be the closure of the business. The Statement of Cash Flows contains the figure for the cash flow from operating activities. The current liabilities are shown on the balance sheet. It is best to use the average current liabilities for at least two years and calculate the average in case there are significant fluctuations in the amount. The formula is

$$\frac{\text{Net cash flow from operating activities}}{\text{Average current liabilities}} \times 100$$

It should ring alarm bells if the company does not have sufficient cash coming in to cover its current liabilities.

Cash Recovery Rate

When a company purchases fixed assets such as machinery or buildings, it is making a long-term investment in the belief that it will generate good future cash flows. We need to determine whether these assets in which we have invested will generate more cash than they cost. To make the calculation, the cash flow figure is taken from the cash flow statement. The assets figure is shown on the balance sheet. Some analysts take the total assets figure of assets, others focus on the fixed assets and not include the value of current assets. In this case, the formula is:

$$\frac{\text{Net cash flow from operations}}{\text{Average total (or less current) assets}} \times 100$$

Cash recovery rate is sometimes used when it is suspected that a company is not financially very healthy. The question arises whether the assets it has can generate more cash than their current worth. In these circumstances, you must be alert to the fact that the value of the asset shown on a company's balance sheet is its original cost less any depreciation charged to date. This, in all probability, is not a guide to the value of the asset on the open market or the cost to replace it.

Cash Flow Per Share

You may be interested in a company that has shares on a stock exchange. You may hold some shares yourself or be contemplating making your own investment. One figure of interest is the amount of cash generated by each share. The company requires a cash surplus to pay a dividend to its shareholders. You can calculate the amount of cash flowing into the company in different ways.

You can extract the amount from the Income Statement by taking the Earnings before interest, tax, depreciation, and amortization (EBITDA) as the "cash flow" amount. If you have access to a cash flow statement, you can take net cash flow from operating activities. If the company has sold any of its assets, it is best to deduct that amount from your calculations. The cash flow will be divided by the weighted number of ordinary shares and the formula is:

$$\frac{\text{Cash flow}}{\text{Weighted number of ordinary shares in issue}}$$

The resulting figure can be compared to other companies or calculated for several years. If the amount of cash flow per share is minimal, you may wish to revise your interest in that company. A low figure suggests that anyone holding ordinary shares is likely to receive only a small dividend. Remember that preference shareholders should receive their fixed percentage dividend before ordinary shareholders see any benefits.

Free Cash Flow Ratio

In addition to paying dividends, there is also an expectation, or hope, that a company may grow and become even more profitable. There is also the concern that the company may not have sufficient cash to survive a difficult economic climate. To answer these concerns, you should identify the operating cash flow. Some analysts deduct capital expenditures from this amount as they argue that these are necessary to maintain the company's activities. The amount of free cash flow you have identified can be compared to previous years using a trend analysis or to other companies. You can also calculate a ratio using the following formula:

$$\frac{\text{Free cash flow}}{\text{Operating cash flow}}$$

If a company has a high percentage of free cash flow, it is interpreted as being financially stable as it has financial strength.

The following example of a summary cash flow is taken from the annual financial report of Barrick Gold Corporation, which is the largest gold mining company in the world, with its headquarters in Canada. Note that this summary is taken from their annual report that contains 176 pages.

https://barrick.com/English/investors/annual-report/default.aspx

Summary of Cash Inflow (Outflow)		
($ millions)		
For the years ended December 31	2018	2017
Net cash provided by operating activities	$ 1,765	$2,065
Investing activities		
Capital expenditures	$ (1,400)	$ (1,396)
Divestitures	990	
Other	(94)	69
Total investing inflows/(outflows)	$ (1,494)	$ (337)
Financing activities		
Net change in debt1	$ (687)	$ (1,533)
Dividends	(125)	(125)
Other	(113)	(228)

Total financing inflows/(outflows)	$ (925)	$ (1,886)
Effect of exchange rate	(9)	3
Increase/(decrease) in cash and equivalents	$ (663)	$ (155)

Notes

1. *The difference between the net change in debt on a cash basis and the net change on the balance sheet is due to changes in non-cash charges, specifically the unwinding of discounts and amortization of debt issue costs.*
2. *In 2018, we declared dividends in US dollars totalling $0.19 per share and paid $0.12 per share (2017: declared and paid $0.12 per share; 2016: declared and paid $0.08 per share)*

Ratio Analysis and Small Businesses

The examples we have given have been mainly from large companies. This is because their financial statements are easily accessible. However, the managers of smaller businesses can benefit substantially by using ratios to monitor their own performance. There are also many people outside the business who may wish to conduct a financial analysis. The bank and the tax authorities are obvious ones. There are also suppliers and customers who may wish to know if their business relationship is on a steady financial basis.

The ratios we have explained earlier in this chapter in respect of large companies can also be used for small businesses. Where you have good access for obtaining the financial statements, you may wish to conduct a simple trend analysis as we demonstrated in Chapter 2. If the financial statements of similar companies can be obtained, the analysis can be improved by a better understanding of the competitors. We would recommend you calculate the ratios for a small business and the guidance on how to interpret them is given below.

Return on Net Assets

We have met this ratio previously when we discussed profitability ratios and the return on capital employed. The calculation is the same but we have used a different title. For some unknown reason, RONA seems usually to be applied for smaller companies. For many companies, a return on net assets is regarded as the main measure of its performance. The company can only improve that ratio by improving the ratios for the contributing activities.

Net Asset Turnover

This is a useful measure to assess whether the company is using its net assets efficiently. The ratio can indicate that some assets are not being fully employed. This will need further investigation. Examples of inefficiencies that may be taking place are machinery being constantly idle or under used land and buildings because they are only partly occupied or too large for the level of activity.

Another avenue may be to increase the sales volume without requiring additional net assets to meet the increased demand. If the company can increase sales without requiring a further investment in net assets, the net asset turnover will improve. The company will have to take some difficult decisions to increase production without investing in more assets.

Gross Profit Margin

This ratio represents the difference between the selling price and the costs of the goods sold. If the gross profit margin is 25 percent, it will be that for one dollar, or $1 million of sales. An increase in the volume of sales will not change the ratio. If the aim is to improve the ratio, it will need an increase in the selling price of items or/and a decrease in their cost.

Return on Sales Ratio

This ratio expresses the profit as a percentage of the sales figure. To improve this ratio, it requires either an increase in the selling price of the products or a reduction of the costs incurred in producing it. An increase in the volume of sales will have to be achieved without the operating costs increasing.

Financial Structure

It is rightly claimed (Pticar 2016) that owners of small businesses need to know their optimal financial structure. Because businesses have their own structure, industry and economic environment, the standard ratios above may not always provide the most useful information to the business owners. The issue is the ratio between the size and structure of assets on one side and the size and structure of equity and debt on the other side. It is important that the entrepreneur maintains a balance between debt and equity and general advice is that the ratio between liabilities and shareholder's equity (debt to equity ratio) should be lower than 1 to 1.

The Economic Environment

If you wish to broaden your analysis, you can find that the local radio stations and newspapers frequently carry news on local businesses. You may even wish to go a stage further and investigate the financial statements of any companies supplying goods or using the small business. If they are having difficulties, then this will be reflected in the performance of the smaller business. If a main supplier is struggling then this may affect the company in which you are interested.

Investment Ratios

This section is mostly concerned with those companies that are listed on a stock exchange. Shareholders are interested in the share price and the return they are receiving on their investment. They can measure their return both in the increase in the share price—a capital gain, and in the dividend they receive.

Although the financial statements may provide information on the company, investors make their decisions on both the financial statements and an analysis of external factors. One term that is frequently used to "measure" companies is *Market Capitalization*. This is calculated to ascertain the value the stock market puts on a company. The formula is:

Current share price × Number of ordinary shares in issue

As share prices fluctuate, even on a daily basis, the "value" of the company is always changing. At no stage is it possible to match the market valuation with the "book value" of the company. You will find that many large companies often have the current share price displayed on their website.

One may spend considerable time calculating ratios and there are several good books and articles that focus specifically on the information needs of the buyer of shares. In this section, we will provide a brief explanation of the various ratios that shareholders can use when deciding on their investments.

Leverage or Gearing Ratios

Both the terms gearing and leverage refer to the same ratio. Leverage or gearing refers to the relative proportions of equity and debt that a company has in its financial structure. The ratio analyzes the financial structure of the business by comparing the amount of equity compared to long-term debt. The ratio indicates the risk attached to the return on the investment. These risks arise because of fluctuations in profit.

Businesses fund their activities with the capital invested by the owners plus any retained earnings giving the amount of total equity. They may also have borrowed funds from banks and other financial institutions and these form the long-term liabilities, frequently referred to as debt.

The relative proportions of equity and debt that a company has in its financial structure has an impact on profit in different economic conditions. A highly leveraged company is one that has a high proportion of debt in relation to equity. In times of increasing profit, this is of great benefit to shareholders. A decline in profits will cause those shareholders grief. A company that has a low proportion of debt in relation to equity is a low leveraged company. This will not be so exciting to shareholders but is less risky when there is an economic downturn.

Interest Cover

A useful ratio that is easy to calculate but can be very informative is interest cover. The purpose of the ratio is to determine the number of times current interest charges can be paid out of current profits before interest and tax. Instead of PBIT, you may see the acronym EBIT meaning Earnings before interest and tax.

$$\frac{\text{Profit (Earnings) before interest and tax}}{\text{Interest charge}} = \text{Number of times}$$

If the interest charge can be paid, that is, it is covered several times from the profit, investors can be confident that they will receive their return. Lenders will receive their interest and existing shareholders should receive some form of dividend.

In an economic downturn, the low leveraged company is less risky than a highly leveraged company. With a highly leveraged company, the number of times that profits can cover interest charges will be very few. If the profits are insufficient to cover the interest charges, the company is insolvent. In the worst situation, there are insufficient profits to cover interest and there is the danger that the company will go into bankruptcy. When the economy is booming, profits are higher and a company can pay its interest charges and a dividend.

The lower the interest cover, the weaker the company's financial position looks. If the company can only pay its interest, shareholders will not receive a dividend. If the interest falls below 1.0, lenders are not going to receive all the interest they are due in that financial period. The company has significant financial problems and it is probable that it will not be able to continue without taking some major actions.

Earnings Per Share

Shareholders are interested in the financial performance of a company as this is a guide to the dividend they may receive. If a company is paying high dividends, the shareholder not only has an immediate return but the share price may increase as it is a successful company.

A company does not usually pay all its profit out as dividends. The aim of the company is to grow and it can do this by retaining some of the profit for expansion. The shareholder may not receive such a high dividend but if the company is growing, the shareholder's shares will be more valuable, that is, there is capital growth.

The basic EPS is calculated by dividing the profit or loss attributable to ordinary equity holders of the parent entity (the numerator) by the weighted average number of ordinary shares outstanding (the denominator) during the period. This is all ordinary shares in issue during the year.

Price/Earnings Ratio (P/E Ratio)

The P/E ratio reflects the stock market's opinion on the possible future earnings of the company. The ratio calculates the number of times it will take the investor to recover the cost of their shares from current profits. The ratio uses the earnings per share and the current market price of one share, the formula being:

$$\frac{\text{Current price of one share in the market}}{\text{Earnings per share}}$$

Dividends Per Share

Dividends are paid from profits. The financial statement shows the total amount paid in dividends. The individual shareholder is more interested in the dividend they receive for each share they hold. The following two ratios can be calculated.

The dividend net.

This is the amount of dividend per share for the financial year.

The dividend yield.

This measures the dividend yielded on a share in relation to the current market price.

Limitations of Ratio Analysis

Managers, investors, lenders, competitors, and others are interested in the financial performance of an organization. In the previous two chapters, we have discussed the providers and users of financial information. In this chapter, we have explained the various ratios one can calculate, but the choice of the analysis method depends on the needs of the user and the availability of the data. This means that the users must first identify the problem. To do this, it can be helpful to calculate the main ratios and to assess whether these provide any clarity to the fundamental problem.

Unfortunately, the data needed to calculate the ratios may not be available. Also, comparative data will be needed. This may not be readily accessible for previous periods (for example, trend analysis is not possible for a new business) or for similar companies in the same industry (for example, if the business operates in a niche market and there are no industry benchmarks).

It must also be remembered that, although financial statements can be revealing, they can also be misleading especially in periods of high inflation. There is also the problem that some form of window dressing may have taken place. Companies, in making public their financial progress, may wish to make a situation look better than it really is and they embark on the practice known as window dressing. If the financial statements have been audited by an independent firm of accountants, this should not occur. However, you should be aware of the risk and also remember that Directors, in providing a commentary on a company's financial performance, may choose to highlight specific achievements and be less forthcoming on failures.

Finally, with all types and sizes of companies, financial statements do not encompass or measure non-financial factors. Not all aspects of a business can be captured by ratio analysis. The analysis of financial statements will not reveal whether a business has sound plans for the future, a good reputation, a strong customer base, reliable suppliers, loyal employees, or strong competitors. Your analysis of the main financial statements will reveal substantial information about the company's performance, but the ratios must be understood in the context in which they are calculated.

Conclusions

In this chapter, we have concentrated on financial statement analysis. We have indicated the financial information available and explained the calculation of ratios and also their analysis and interpretation. In analyzing ratios, you need comparisons so that you can draw conclusions. The comparisons may be the financial statements of one company over several years. It may be the statements of other companies.

Companies, of any size, must produce financial statements. Assuming that they are "for profit" organizations, at least the taxation authorities will require them as well as the owners of the business. An analysis of these financial statements will reveal considerable insights into a company's performance. If you are interested in large companies, you will find the information easy to obtain and you can become overwhelmed by the amount that is available.

Our explanations have concentrated on profitability, liquidity, and efficiency, and cash management. To do this, we have explained the purpose and content of three financial statements: the income statement that shows profit or loss, the balance sheet that contains information on all the assets and liabilities and, finally, the cash flow statement. The ratios are extremely helpful in understanding the financial performance and standing of a company.

Whatever the type of organization, you must know the regulations that have been applied in constructing them. You may be interested in smaller organizations, possibly one that you own or work for, or a competitor. In all probability, the financial statements should comply with the regulation in the country in which it operates. If you are interested in larger companies, you must ascertain whether the company is complying with its own country's standards, International Financial Reporting Standards, or standards issued by the U.S. Financial Accounting Standards Board.

Action Plan

To apply your analytical knowledge, you need to identify your objectives. Are you interested in the profitability of the company, the value of the assets and liabilities, or the cash reserves, if there are any? Financial statement analysis is essential to give the "big picture." However, the financial statements, no matter how carefully you conduct your analysis, do not provide you with the detail. To do this, you need to obtain the management accounting information that the company uses to manage its business. Such information is not publicly available, but depending on your need for the information it may be possible to access it.

In the next chapter, we explain the different management accounting methods that companies use. We explain the different types of costs a company can incur and the methods it uses to manage all activities it undertakes. The methods it uses can depend on the nature of the company's activities. Making computers is a very different activity to erecting a building or providing some form of transport service.

If you have decided in Chapter 1 that you are interested in a particular company or type of industry, in Chapter 4, you will find guidance to the types of financial information they use internally to manage their activities.

Before you start on Chapter 4, you will find it useful to collect as much information available on a particular industry or company. Use the methods of analysis we have described in this chapter to give you the "big picture." This provides the foundation for taking a more detailed analysis.

CHAPTER 4

Management Decision Making

About This Chapter

In the previous chapter, we concentrated on financial accounting, which is concerned with the performance and position of the entire organization. Business success, however, depends on the detailed information that is available to managers so that they can make decisions, investigate problems, set performance targets, and carry out their responsibilities of managing an organization or a part of it.

It is the responsibility of managers to plan and control activities whether this is for a division, branch, or a specific activity. To do this successfully, a manager requires detailed information in a timely manner to make appropriate decisions. Managers need data that is relevant to their responsibilities and that is received in time for them to take action. They also need to understand the definitions used in relation to the costs of various activities and feel confident in analyzing that cost information.

Managers are interested in issues such as the costs of operating a particular activity, making a specific article, operating different types of machinery, and selecting different methods of working. Understanding the components of cost and being able to use them assists managers in controlling the operations and activities on a daily basis, to plan for the future, and to decide on alternative courses of action. In this chapter, we concentrate on the different costing methods and techniques that are available and are used in various industries and circumstances.

Cost or Management Accounting

From the days that businesses started operating, the owners and managers would keep some basic accounting records. As the years passed, a body of techniques and methods were established that went under the general heading of cost accounting. In the United States, in 1919, a meeting of accountants was held and the National Association of Cost Accountants (NACA) was formed. This was later to become the Institute of Management Accountants with a membership of 125,000 (Parks 2019).

The term "cost" accounting refers to the actual methods and techniques for identifying the total costs of each part of productive activity. These results are usually compared to the past or planned results. Management accounting is reporting the results to internal managers. This may be on a monthly, weekly, or in some instances, on a daily basis. The terms are sometimes used interchangeably but both manufacturing and service organizations use cost/management accounting.

It is important to emphasize that, unlike financial accounting, there are no regulations requiring organizations to use cost/management accounting and organizations do so because of the very useful information it generates for managers. The dominant characteristics of cost/management accounting are:

- It is collected, collated, and communicated to managers for planning, control, and decision making.
- It is intended for an internal audience and it is a voluntary system implemented by an organization to meet its own needs.
- There are no regulations controlling the cost information an organization uses.
- There are several techniques that fall under the heading of cost accounting. An organization uses the techniques that best meets its needs, and may revise and refine the technique, if necessary, to be applicable to its own detailed operations.
- Management accounting information is private to the organization and usually is not publicly available.

If you are examining a company's management accounting records, you will find that it is focused on the costs incurred by the organization when conducting its activities. This is because until you know the cost of a product or service, you cannot set the selling price and earn a profit.

The term "cost" can be used in many different situations and the definition of cost can depend on the nature of activities. The best place to start is by identifying what we mean when we ask what "it" costs whether it is a product or service. The accounting term used to identify the "it" is "cost object."

The Cost Object

A cost object is anything for which cost data is required. This may be the sales manager wanting to know the costs of running the sales department. The production manager may be interested in the total cost in one unit of production. The transport manager wants to know the costs of delivering goods to specific locations.

All these managers have different information needs that the costing system in an organization attempts to satisfy. However, this requires collecting and analyzing the information that is available and, in some cases, collecting additional information. This can be an expensive process so decisions need to be made on the importance of the information to management.

Having identified the cost object, you need to identify the different types of costs that are involved with that particular object. The main classifications are direct material costs, direct labor costs, and indirect costs also referred to as overheads.

In a manufacturing industry, the direct costs of materials and labor are usually easy to identify. Records will be available to show the cost of materials used and the cost of wages for those working on production. Usually, the direct costs vary in line with production activity. Records will be kept of labor hours and material usage. In a service industry, it can be more difficult in identifying the direct costs incurred.

Total direct costs vary with activity levels. There may be an occasional increase in the costs of materials or a wage rise. These are one-off increases and we will have to take them into our calculations. However, the main reason for direct costs fluctuating is activity levels. The more you make, the more the total cost.

Indirect costs (overheads) include the costs of running the organization and tend to be fixed and do not change by activity levels although there may be other reasons, for example, the provider of the services such as insurance and government charges are usually increased by the supplier without reference to the user. The critical issue in all types of industry is the method to be applied to share the total overhead costs for the organization over the various activities and the cost objects generated within one financial period.

Direct Costs

These types of costs can be identified with a specific cost object, which may be a particular product, service, department, or other cost object. Examples are raw materials used in production and labor costs where they can be traced to that particular activity.

In a manufacturing organization, materials that can be identified directly with the product are likely to be significant. The increasing use of mechanization and robotics has, in some industries, reduced the amount of direct labor required. But be cautious: in some industries, where skilled labor is an essential part of the manufacturing process, the cost can be high. There is also the possibility that where machinery is introduced to replace labor, there the depreciation cost on the machinery will be a fixed cost.

Generally, in service industries, direct labor will be high and material costs low or even insignificant. An accounting firm doing a major audit will have high direct labor costs incurred by the people doing the audit but practically zero direct material costs.

Calculating the cost of direct materials to specific cost objects can cause difficulties. These fall under two headings: the practical and the price. On a practical basis, good records and work procedures are essential to ensure that wastage of materials does not occur, as any wastage represents a cost that should be avoided. An organization should ensure that materials ordered are correctly received from the suppliers, stored in safe and secure conditions, and only issued when required by production. This usually safeguards the processing of the correct quantity of materials.

The delivery of materials may take place over a period of time, and this does not necessarily synchronize with the quantities being issued to production. Prices will therefore vary over that period of time due to factors such as:

- Inflation or deflation giving rise to price changes
- Variations in exchange rates if materials are purchased overseas
- Shortages in the supply of materials, leading to price increases
- Temporary reductions due to such factors as special offers and discounts

Different methods can be used for determining the price of the materials issued to production. Of course, the method chosen for issues to production also affects the value of the closing inventory. This amount will be shown on the financial statements, and financial accounting standards determine which methods are acceptable, as explained in Chapter 2. Most companies will select a method that meets the requirements of the financial accounting standard and also establishes a cost that is useful for management. Whatever method is used, the overriding requirement for financial accounting is that inventory should be valued at the lower of its cost and the net realizable value (i.e., the amount it could be sold for less the costs of selling).

The cost of direct labor is usually based on the remuneration system used in the company. It is essential that a sound record system is in place to charge the correct cost of labor to the appropriate activity. For example, in a manufacturing organization, piecework tickets or swipe cards may be used to record the times of different types of labor at various stages of the production process. Time sheets are widely used in the manufacturing and service industries. For example, employees in accounting or law firms will record their billable hours for each client's job.

Indirect Costs

In addition to those direct costs that can be identified with the production or service activity, there are also indirect costs. These cannot be identified with an individual cost object as they may be organizational or departmental wide. For example, supervisor salaries, heating in the buildings, and telephone costs, which in many organizations can be higher than the direct costs. Frequently, these indirect costs or overheads can be grouped under the following headings:

- Production overheads
- Administration overheads
- Selling overheads

Depending on the nature of the organization's activities, there may also be distribution overheads and research and development overheads. In some organizations, the distribution cost of a particular product can be significant and identified directly with the job. Research costs are usually regarded as overheads but for a large project, these may be considered direct.

In a service organization, the overheads can be substantial. If you stay in a hotel, the costs of cleaning your room and the complimentary breakfast are insignificant. It is the property tax for the hotel site, the depreciation charge on fixtures, furniture and equipment, lighting and heating, and the hotel staff you see, such as the employees at the front desk. These are the indirect costs of running the hotel. These indirect costs will tend to remain the same irrespective of changes in the level of activity.

Fixed and Variable Costs

Fixed costs refer to those costs that stay the same in total regardless of changes in levels of activity but can change either upwards or downwards for other reasons. For example, the local government may raise the tax it charges on properties. This is nothing to do with activity levels and the nature of the cost is still regarded as fixed.

Although the fixed cost *in total* remains the same for the financial period, the fixed cost *per unit* can change as activity levels change, as the following example shows.

Example of changes in fixed costs

Endow manufactures and installs children's slides. The Factory Manager cannot understand why the total cost of manufacturing a slide changes throughout the year. The Accountant explains that the fixed cost is $18,000 in total for the financial year. This must be paid regardless of changes in activity.

The information is given to the manager on a monthly basis. As the fixed costs do not fluctuate depending on the activity levels, the fixed cost per month is calculated as $18,000/12 = $1,500 per month. However, production levels fluctuate throughout the year. This means that the fixed cost per unit can change each month. She demonstrates this with the following Table 4.1.

Table 4.1 Fixed cost behavior with fluctuating activity levels

	January	February	March
Fixed cost	$1,500	$1,500	$1,500
Number of slides	10	30	50
Fixed cost per slide	$150	$50	$30

The Marketing Manager says that this seems unfair but the Accountant responds that the Factory Manager is responsible for ensuring efficient output and not for the total fixed cost. Although the fixed cost **in total** remains the same for the financial period, the variable costs are the costs that change in total as activity changes. In their organization, the variable costs were essentially labor and materials. These were budgeted at $100 slide. Using the above example of activity levels, the variable costs are shown in the following Table 4.2.

Table 4.2 Variable cost behavior with fluctuating activity levels

	January	February	March
Variable cost per slide	$100	$100	$100
Number of slides	10	30	50
Total variable cost	$1000	$3000	$5000

The different behaviors of fixed and variable costs need to be borne in mind when you are attempting to analyze financial information.

A manager can only lower the fixed cost per unit by achieving maximum activity levels. The variable cost per unit is dependent on the controls that are placed on costs that vary with levels of activity. Materials consumed in production being the prime example.

The problem of fixed costs is where there is a significant downturn in business. A company can observe its activity levels decreasing and also the direct costs, but the fixed costs are likely to remain the same. Unless a solution can be found, this leads to bankruptcy of the company.

The Industry Perspective

There is no legislation for companies to do management accounting. Companies can therefore choose which method of costing to adopt or decide to not have a management accounting system, but this would be unusual. Not only does an organization choose the method of costing it will use but also how frequently the system will generate information for the managers. Usually, it will be no more than monthly that the management information is available, although some companies have weekly reporting. On key activities, there may even be daily reporting of the main figures.

Different types of industries will select the costing method that provides the financial information to help them manage. The main distinction is between service companies and manufacturing companies. From your own experience, you will appreciate that these are very different industries with different functions and outputs. In this section, we consider the distinctive features, as far as costing is concerned for each industry.

The Service Sector

A simple definition of the service sector is difficult as it covers such a range of activities from hairdressers, concert halls, auto repair shops, and banks. There is no specific method of costing designed exclusively for organizations in the service sector. This is not to argue that the costing methods used in the service and manufacturing sectors are exactly the same. However, the two industries are very different and the service industry has specific issues to resolve if it is attempting to introduce a costing system.

Service organizations usually have little inventory and the distinction between costs related to the product and costs related to a financial period may not be relevant. It is difficult to separate service organizations' costs into their fixed and variable elements. Specific costs are not easily traceable to certain revenue or output items. Finally, a substantial share of the costs are overhead costs, which are usually more difficult to categorize than direct costs.

In service organizations where an easily identifiable cost object can be devised or where there are identifiable jobs, the procedures we have explained in this chapter can be applied for the allocation of overheads and the calculation of an allocation rate. Remember that a cost object may not be a physical item such as a tire for a car. It may be that a cost object has to be generated, which is hypothetical and not physical. For example, a hotel may decide on an occupied bed night as a cost object. Their need is to know how much it costs to let a room for one night. A transport company may develop a hybrid measure combining weight and distance kilometers. The company will know how much it costs to transport a certain weight of material for one kilometer.

Although costing in the service sector can cause problems, most companies will have some form of budgetary control system. This may be a basic system but provides management with targets they should meet and how successful they were in meeting these targets. We explain budgetary control later in this chapter.

The Manufacturing Sector

In the manufacturing sector, there is normally an identifiable product or products. The company may make only one product or several products. It may be that the product has to go through various stages of manufacture. The product is partially made in one process, then moves on to the next process for more work to be carried out. The finished output at one stage of production becomes the input for the next stage. Each stage or process can usually be clearly identified and is often contained in a separate department.

Where the product has to move through various processes, management usually wants to know the costs that are involved at each stage.

It is this detailed knowledge that helps managers to make decisions and identify issues arising from a particular stage of production. If management is keeping a close watch on the costs at each stage of production, it may concentrate only on direct costs as indirect costs remain the same irrespective of the level of activity.

It is usually possible to identify the direct costs. There will be material costs, which can be very expensive in some companies, and labor costs although these have become less important in some sectors of industry as mechanization has become more advanced. There is a problem that occurs at the end of each financial period. We know the number of units completed during the financial period but a number of cost objects are not completed and will progress to the next period. For financial accounting, we need to know the cost of these incomplete units but these are usually not so important for management accounting information. What may be important is how many incomplete units there are and the reason for this.

Types of Costing

Manufacturing and service industries are very different and the types of costing they use mirrors these differences. However, one of the most frequent questions used when making any decisions in either industry is "What did it cost?" The answer will depend on the industry you are in, the size of the organization, and the purpose for wanting this information. Not surprisingly, several costing methods have evolved and in this section we consider these.

There are no regulations controlling the nature of the accounting information that is used specifically by managers to manage an organization. However, it is essential that the system of cost accounting generates data that is useful and at the end of a financial period and does not give figures that are significantly at variance with the legally required financial accounts.

In this section, we are providing a general view of the different types of costing methods. Organizations will modify, adapt, and change the method to suit their own particular needs. What they will find is that all the methods are "costly" to operate but without the information a well-designed system provides, you cannot plan, measure, and benefit from your work.

Process Costing

Process costing method is normally used where the manufacturing is conducted in a series of separate stages until there is the final product that can be sold. In some organizations, there may be more than one final product. For example, a company may make a standard model and add something to it so that it also has a "superior model" for sale at a higher price.

Where there is only one final product, the costs of each of the separate processes are identified for a specific period and divided by the output to give an average cost per unit. Direct costs for a process can be identified from the accounting records and overheads will be allocated to the separate processes. A company may collect only the information on direct costs as the indirect costs will remain the same. The average cost of each cost unit can be calculated at each stage by simply dividing the total cost of that process for a period of time by the number of cost units produced in that period. The costs for the cost units are aggregated to give the final total cost for all of the processes that production goes through.

Often there is not one single product. There will be a main product, joint products, and by-products. It is further complicated by calculating the value of work in progress at the end of the financial period and accounting for normal and abnormal losses that have occurred during the production process.

The work in progress at the end of the first stage of production means those units are still incomplete and have to be finished before they can be transferred to stage 2. These are incomplete units but we need to put a value on them. These units will also incur additional costs in the next financial period so that the units are complete.

Process Costing Example

To demonstrate the application of process costing, we will assume that we are concerned with stage 1, which is January. There are several pieces of information we require at the end of January. We want to know the cost of the completed units, the costs of any normal or abnormal losses and, most importantly, how much it has cost us in January in Process 1 to produce incomplete units, which are referred to as work in process (WIP). If, at the end of January, there were 10,000 units that had been only 50 percent completed, we would say that these were the equivalent of 5,000 completed units. If the cost of a completed unit is $0.50, so the cost of our 10,000 incomplete units is 10,000 × $.50 = $5,000.

This may seem a somewhat inexact way of calculating the costs of incomplete units but we have what is known as "The cost of costing." Generating financial information is expensive and management must decide how much information they require to make decisions. Assuming that the production process is well managed, the method of costing for processes is fairly straightforward and giving time and attention to the costs of incomplete units on a monthly basis may not be of use to everyday management. It is important for financial accounting where it is essential to identify the full cost of the products and the value of the closing inventory.

Job Costing

Manufacturing and service organizations carrying out work that has been specifically requested need to know the cost of each individual job, as this will be related to the selling price. Job costing, also known as specific order costing, is the accounting method used by such organizations. Whether a quote has to be provided for painting the outside of a domestic residence or for building a bridge across a river, control of costs is essential. The purpose of the method is to "quote" the cost of a job, whether it involves a tangible product or a particular service for a client. The quote is based not only on all the costs for doing the job but also a measure of profit. This is not usually disclosed to the customer.

Jobs are usually identified as a piece of work, carried out to a customer's specific requirements. A company taking on a job can record the direct costs, such as materials and labor but there are also the overhead costs such as administration, advertising, and depreciation on equipment.

Jobs can be very small and of short duration such as having the local garage servicing your car or a company decorating your house. The garage and the decorators will want to keep control of their costs so that they make a profit. The garage will have its fixed costs, as explained above, but there will be the variable costs of the mechanic's time and the materials that are used.

Some jobs can be very big and take months to complete. Jobs such as building a new factory or building a bridge over a river will require material and labor but also heavy machinery that will be used on several different jobs. On these long-term jobs, it is essential that the accountant and the manager in charge of the job communicate, as work is processed.

With all the jobs, the provider of the service or product need to maintain control of the costs incurred in doing the job to ensure that there is a profit to be gained. Usually, each job is specific to the client. The time it takes to do the job is critical and is recognized as the cost object. To ensure a project is profitable, the provider will need to control its direct costs such as labor and materials. However, it will also need to have a method for charging overheads to the job.

In some industries, it is sometimes possible to negotiate the price of a job on a cost-plus policy. The final selling price is calculated by adding an agreed fixed-profit margin to the cost of the job. This approach has a number of weaknesses, as there is no incentive to control the cost of the job. It ignores market conditions, and the total costs are dependent on the method of overhead recovery. If a client does enter into such a contract, it is essential that the job specification is agreed in minute detail.

Job Costing Example

Home Protect is a small enterprise and designs and installs security systems for domestic and commercial buildings. It manufactures the security system itself to meet the requirements of the purchaser. It pays its direct labor $10 per hour and there is the cost of the materials. It adds 15 percent to the production cost of the job to cover the administration and selling costs (the overheads). It also adds 20 percent to the installation costs for overheads. It has been requested to submit a quote for a security system for a private dwelling. It calculates its costs as follows.

	$
Costs for manufacturing system	
Material	1,250
Labor (30 hours @ $10 per hour)	300
	1,550
Manufacturing overheads ($1,550 × 15%)	235
	1,785
Costs for installation	
Labor (12 hours @ $10 per hour)	120
Installation overheads ($120 × 20%)	25
	1,930

Home Protection gives a quote of $2,500

Your first reaction on seeing this quote (which will not be shown to the potential customer) is that there are errors in the additions. Remember that this is a quote and Home Protection are not certain that the customer will accept it. The calculations are generally close and the quote given allows Home Protection some bargaining leeway if it wants the job. Remember. Home Protection still has to meet the costs of its own premises, advertising, and salaries of staff, in other words, the overheads.

Good accounting can be extremely helpful. To achieve absolute precision can be expensive and we sometimes have to judge if precise management accounting data is worth the cost in generating it. Even with financial accounting, we do not expect companies to report to the nearest dollar. Refer back to Chapter 3 and you will see that financial accounts, which are legally required, may be drawn up to the nearest one million dollars.

Where the final selling price is calculated by adding an agreed fixed-profit margin to the cost of the job, there are a number of weaknesses, as there is no incentive to control the cost of the job. It ignores market conditions, and the total costs are dependent on the method of overhead recovery. If a client does enter into such a contract, it is essential that the job specification is agreed in minute detail.

Where the jobs are specifically designed for one customer, job costing can provide managerial advantages. It provides controls on the operations. In the case of Home Protection, the hours the job is expected to take. It is a basis for improving quotations in the future. Finally, in some industries, certain jobs are so repetitive and financially minor that the company does not need to cost each job. Everyday examples are oil changes for your car and visits to the hair dresser. Although there is a customer (yourself) and the job is specifically for you, the service provider usually has a standard price based on previous experience. This "average" cost is deemed sufficiently precise in management accounting terms.

Full Costing or Absorption Costing

In recent years, there have been suggestions to calculate the full costs of an organization's activities. The full cost would include social, environmental, and economic costs. The traditional accounting approach is therefore expanded to include costs that make up what is referred to as the triple bottom line, a term introduced by John Elkington (1997). We will examine these developments in Chapter 6 but in this chapter, we explain "full costing," without including these other costs, although we do not deny their importance.

Full costing, also known as absorption costing or traditional costing, is usually linked to the manufacturing sector of industry. The purpose of this method is to identify and to value the material, labor, and overhead costs incurred to provide a product or service. The method was developed in the manufacturing sector and reflects the priorities of production facilities.

In calculating the cost of an object, the material and labor costs present no major problems. There will be a system in place to record the costs incurred on a regular basis. We have the problem of factory overheads. These cannot be directly identified with a single product but relate to the entire output. As we explained earlier in this chapter, although the output may fluctuate, the fixed costs in total remain the same. Examples of such costs are:

- Depreciation and maintenance costs of machinery
- Maintenance, insurance rates, and power
- Supervision, cleaning, general building repairs

These indirect costs must be added to the direct or prime costs to ascertain the total production cost, also known as factory cost or total factory cost of finished goods. If these total costs are deducted from the sales figure, we will know the manufacturing profit, or loss if that is the case. We emphasize that we are only calculating the profit for the manufacturing process. There will be other costs at the company level.

A manufacturing account will be similar to the following outline:

Manufacturing Account for the Period Ended	
Direct materials (Opening stock + purchases – closing stock)	X
Direct wages	X
Direct expenses	X
Factory overheads	X
Factory (prime) cost	X

Although the above statement requires substantial data collection and analysis, it does not analyze all the costs incurred. We have to make adjustments for any work in progress at the start of the period and any work in progress at the end of the period. There may also be some difficulties in deciding which costs are "factory" costs and which are company costs. However, this information can be expensive to collect and is required only if it helps managers to make decisions.

In our example, we have used only one production center. There could be more than one such center in the same building or factory. A company may have two or more factories with the main management being in a completely separate building. If this is the case, we have to share the total overheads of the organization over the various production cost centers. For example, the costs of cleaning, lighting, heating, and insurance need to be charged in some way to each production department. The procedure usually followed is to charge those overheads to the department that causes them. If there is more than one production center, the remaining overheads are shared over all the centers.

Our example above gives the cost of manufacturing for a period of time. What we need to know is the total manufacturing cost of one item we are manufacturing. Although we have shared the overheads for the entire factory, we need to charge an appropriate amount to the cost object, that is, the articles we are making. There are several ways of doing this. Three methods that are used frequently are:

The Cost Object

Assuming that we are making only one type of product, we can divide the department overheads by the number of units going through that department. This gives an average overhead cost per unit.

Labor Hour Rate

It may be that there are two or more different types of objects manufactured. The overhead costs can be divided by the total hours of manufacturing to give an hourly rate for manufacturing. Note that this is *not* the direct labor cost but the share of overheads cost and is added to the direct costs to give the total production cost.

Machine Hour Rate

The production process may be highly mechanized. In this scenario, you would charge the overheads to the cost object on the basis of the machine hours incurred.

Activity-Based Costing (ABC)

Full costing, although it provides a substantial amount of information to assist decision making, involves considerable arbitrary decisions on cost allocation. It may be that the amount of work required and the nature of the organization's activities make full costing difficult to apply. An alternative method is available known as Activity Based Costing.

Kaplan and Bruns (1987) posited the first treatise of activity-based costing as an alternative to full costing. Their suggestions explained the value of this alternative accounting method in the manufacturing sector. This was particularly helpful as there were indications that, in some areas of manufacturing, the proportion of the direct costs was falling and the indirect costs were increasing.

It is difficult to determine the benefits of ABC rather than Full Costing. Many claims have been made on its application in industry and various studies have been conducted to assess its usage. The results suggest that the claims made on using this method are higher than the actual rate of adoption. White, Anistal, and Anistal (2015) referred to the ABC Paradox as the actual adoption of the system did not match the somewhat extravagant claims made for its usefulness. Our opinion is that companies devise, structure, and implement any method of data collection and analysis to meet their own current information needs. In doing this, they carefully analyze the costs of operating the method.

You may encounter different methods of Full Costing and Activity Based Costing than the "book methods" we describe. Usually, the methods we have described and variations on them are there to meet the information needs of the managers. Most methods will treat direct costs as we have described above. It is in deciding how to account for overheads where there are differences.

With both the main methods and their variations, companies tend to use predetermined overheads. These will be the budgeted total costs for rent, insurance, electricity, power, and other indirect costs because the company cannot wait for the actual amounts, some of which may not be known until the end of the financial year.

The purpose of ABC, as with full costing, is to determine the total cost of a product, service, or activity. ABC differs from Full Costing as it uses the concept of "cost pools." Instead of allocation rates to charge overheads to the products, what is known as "cost drivers" are identified.

The main activities in the organization are classified as cost pools. These could be the existing functional departments or areas where there is considerable activity and cost expenditure. ABC has been criticized and Kaplan, Anderson, and Stevens (2004) proposed a simplified ABC. Undoubtedly, companies if they are considering adopting ABC, are going to design a system that provides the information they need at a cost they are willing to bear.

We have described the two methods used but it is important to remember that companies use costing techniques to meet their own information needs. This collection and analysis of data can be very expensive. There is no legislation that forces an organization to use management accounting.

These discussions on the use or non-use of ABC and its application in companies support the statement we made in Chapter 1. Financial accounting is strongly regulated and companies follow these regulations. Management accounting is not regulated and it is companies' decisions that shape the system they use.

Budgetary Control

There are very few organizations that would not be using some form of budgetary control, no matter how basic it is. A budget is a quantitative or a financial statement prepared before the start of a trading or financial period. This could be a month or a year. The budgets are for a specific time period and set out the business goals to be met during that period. The budget may be for the entire organization but it is normal to also set budgets for different departments or activities.

Even a small organization may construct a simple budget for a year. With larger companies, it is usually divided into smaller periods of a month. Budgets, at least at the top level, are usually in financial terms but non-monetary measures may also be used for separate departments. This could be the sales quotas to be achieved or the number of products to be manufactured in the period. A sales budget would usually have an analysis of the total sales revenue projections. The analysis may be by product, market, advertising and promotion costs, and individuals' sales targets.

It is essential that the budgets for individual sections of the organization are coordinated. It is useless to produce a sophisticated sales budget showing the trend of sales through the period without keying in to other budgets. The manufacturing section will need to know the requirements and the transport section. It will also entail the purchasing department to ensure that the materials are available at the appropriate time and price.

At the end of a budget period, whether this be a month or a week, the actual achievements are measured and compared with the budget. Differences, known as variances, between the budget and actual performance should be investigated.

If you are investigating the performance of an organization or examining the management of a specific function, it is essential that you review any budget that has been prepared and the actual results achieved. Too often, budgets take an optimistic view and the test of its worth is the actual results that are achieved and, where appropriate, the reasons they vary from the budget.

Standard Costing

Standard costing establishes the costs to be incurred. It is used to provide managers with a reporting method and to provide control over costs. The organization determines planned levels of expenditure and income and the actual costs are recorded. The difference between what has been planned and what was achieved is a variance that probably requires investigation to determine the reasons for the difference. Standard costing is usually used for individual products and processes and is frequently used in manufacturing.

The basic concept of the technique is that a cost has been predetermined and the actual cost is compared with it. The difference between the two amounts is known as a variance. If the actual cost is higher than the predetermined standard, the difference is known as an adverse variance. If the actual costs are lower, it is a favorable variance. We will demonstrate the application of standard costing for both direct materials and direct wages. The following diagram illustrates the connections.

Standard Costing – Direct Variables

The bottom line of the diagram is where the main interest lies. Essentially, it gives the answers to the four following questions.

1. Did we pay employees more or less per hour than we intended?
2. Did the employees complete as much work as planned?

```
┌─────────────────────────────┐
│  Total standard cost compared│
│      to total actual cost    │
└─────────────────────────────┘
```

| Labor variances | | Materials variances |

| Rate of Pay Variance | Efficiency variance | Price variance | Usage variance |

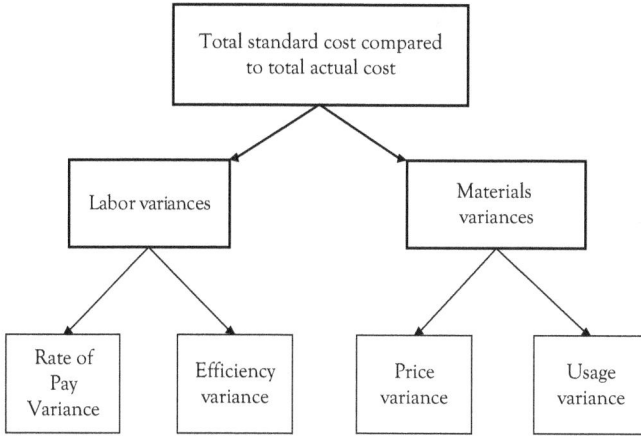

3. Did we pay more per unit of material than we expected?
4. Did we use more material in manufacturing than was planned?

You will find that most manufacturing organizations, whatever their size, will have some standard costing system. It may be scribbled in a notebook or be a computerized system. The purpose is the same—it provides managers with information so that they can manage more successfully.

Conclusions

In this chapter, we have explained the techniques and methods that can be used to help managers make their organization successful. Unlike financial accounting, there are no rules or regulations that lay down what companies must do. A management accounting system can be expensive to operate. Unless it provides useful financial information to managers, it is not worth undertaking. However, there are some business activities, unless they are very small, where only the material costs and direct labor are important. Overheads can be substantial and greatly increase the total costs of your products and services.

There are different approaches to calculate what a product or service costs. The first step is to determine the classification of the costs that are being incurred. We have considered the characteristics of direct costs and indirect costs. We have also explained the main costing methods used by organizations to ensure efficiency.

Having explained the techniques and methods available, in the next chapter, we explain how you can apply this knowledge.

Action Plan

We have given a broad view of the various methods and techniques used for management decision making. The processes we have explained can be applied, in many forms, to most organizations, even the smallest ones. A good example is a simple service such as hair dressing, car cleaning, and other activities carried out by one person with few materials used. The costs incurred in carrying out the activity will be essentially for labor and the overhead costs for operating the business. If you are examining a particular organization, the steps are:

1. Determine which industry it is in. Bear in mind that some organizations have interests in both manufacturing and service.
2. Consider their processes and determine which of the types of costing we have explained is the best fit.
3. Identify which costs are variable and which are fixed.
4. If possible, obtain details of their management accounting system.
5. Compare the methods they use with our descriptions and explain any differences.

CHAPTER 5

Applying Your Knowledge

About This Chapter

In the previous chapter, we explained the different costing methods that can be used to assess the financial functioning of an organization. In this chapter, we demonstrate how you can select the appropriate methods to obtain the financial information you need. You may be the owner of a small business, in partnership, or a manager in a large business. Whatever your role, you are most likely to be interested or significantly involved in the financial success of the business and this chapter provides guidance.

The methods and techniques that we explain in this chapter are not set in stone. You do not change your business to fit into a particular method we have explained. You look carefully at your business, select the methods and techniques that seem to be most helpful, and then tailor them to meet the needs of the business and your aspirations.

Before you determine the information needed, it has to be decided where the business is going. The first section of this chapter deals with the objectives for the business. The considerations will involve the planned profit, and consequently, sales objectives and cost strategies. We explain the various costing methods that may be useful and complete the chapter by discussing activity based and total quality management.

Setting Objectives

The Business Plan

In the previous chapter, we introduced the concept of budgetary control. For a business to be successful, you need a business plan and this will involve some form of budgetary control. A business of any size will usually have a formal budgetary control system. Even a small business directed and controlled by one person, usually the owner, needs some form of business objective even if it has not been formally put on paper. The objectives may be decided solely by the owner and the achievement, or otherwise, of these objectives is the responsibility of the owner. In larger businesses, where you are a manager, you may have responsibility for part of the business plan.

As a business expands, there is a growth in the organization and this will necessitate the division of responsibilities. These divisions or sections usually are the responsibility of specialist managers. There may be a sales manager, a purchasing manager, and in a manufacturing organization, a specialist manager in charge of that section. It is essential that the separate managers know the business objectives and the progress toward these are discussed regularly.

In a large organization, the business plan is no longer determined by an owner. Many of the day-to-day decisions will be made by the line managers. These decisions must be made within an overall plan, which will be the master budget. The business will have a formal planning and control system, which states the objectives of the business and those of the individual managers of the various sections. There will be a reporting system, usually monthly, which informs the business executives of the financial performance for that month. This report may be available to all the managers or they may receive information that deals only with their specific responsibility.

Small family businesses may experience some difficulty in determining a business plan. It is argued that they experience difficulties in taking the long-term view and do not plan further than establishing yearly budgets. This may also apply to some larger businesses and it is often valuable to use outside experts to assist in establishing a business plan for five years or more, if needed.

Sales and Production Budgets

One of the purposes of preparing budgets is to coordinate activities. There is no value of having a sales budget if the manufacturing department cannot produce the number or type of items required. The value of monthly budgets is they ensure that sales and production volumes are coordinated, thus preventing product shortages or overstocking. To ensure that this coordination occurs, it is usual to prepare budgets not only in financial terms but also in numbers. For a manufacturing industry, budgets are usually produced both in financial terms and by volumes. An example is the budget of a sales manager. The amount of revenue will be measured not only in financial terms but also in quantitative terms. This information will be connected to the data in the manufacturing budget.

It is essential that there is coordination of budgets for the operations. The sales and production budgets when coordinated will show the finished stock budget to be constructed. The manager of the distribution unit will prepare a budget by considering the following factors:

- The volume of units to be delivered and the locations
- The number of kilometers involved
- The costs of delivery depending on gas prices
- The costs of repairs and maintenance

Undoubtedly, in an uncertain business environment, there can be difficulty in establishing budgets, but if you have no plans on where you want to go, you have no foundation on where to direct your activities. Budgets are not carved in stone, and circumstances may occur that necessitate a review of the budgets.

Profit and Cash

A key section of the budget is the target profit. The budget profit calculation is simply the difference between the budgeted sales figure and the budgeted costs. Most organizations will draw up their sales budget and purchases budget but if the profit is unacceptable, it means reviewing those two budgets.

It is important to remember that all functional budgets, including both the sales and production budgets, use an accruals basis. This means that the recorded income from sales and the expenditure in the production budgets (and all the other budgets) are recorded when they are generated and not when cash is paid or received. It is therefore essential to draw up a separate cash budget. This will involve taking all the transactions recorded in the sales and production budgets and show them in the Cash Budget in the months that cash is expected to be received or paid.

If a business is seeking additional finance for its activities, a cash budget is an essential document required by any prospective lender.

Budgetary Control

Constructing budgets can be time consuming and it is essential that the budgets are not merely speculations but are used to control and reschedule activities. Budgets are plans for the future activities of a business and also a means of comparing actual performance with the planned performance. There are likely to be differences between actual and plan and these are known as "variances." A favorable variance is where the actual performance is better than the budgeted. With costs, this would mean that the actual costs are lower than the budgeted and with sales the actual sales receipts are better than budgeted.

It is essential to investigate any differences between actual and budgeted performance fully and the problems identified. For example, the results for a financial period may show that the expenditure on materials was higher than budgeted. This may not be a fault of the production manager but it may be that the purchasing manager chose cheaper materials. Although this would have appeared as a favorable variance on the purchasing variance, the result may have been that more materials were used than originally planned.

Comparisons on budgeted costs help managers to make decisions to improve the performance of their organization or the part for which they have the responsibility. However, there are other ways of making comparisons that do not involve the time and expense in constructing budgets. The costs you have presently incurred can be compared with:

- Actual costs in previous periods, but this may obscure the errors and deficiencies in the previous period
- The costs if we chose alternative methods of production, such as outsourcing, using different methods, recruiting lower paid employees.
- If possible, the costs incurred by other organizations.
  This information may be very difficult to acquire.

- Conducting business activities in another country. This may give closer access to the raw materials, have lower wage costs or there could be taxation benefits.

In Chapter 3, we explained standard setting, and you will probably be involved in this activity in the organization where you work. There may be a system of standard costing or of budgetary control or both. Planning future costs is a major part of these costing techniques.

Calculating the Cost

Cost is a difficult term and has different meanings depending on the situation and with different activities. The key question is what is being "costed." The first aspect to determine is whether we are concerned with the costs where the activities are manufacturing or where they are service related. Although there are similarities, there are significant differences in determining the cost.

Manufacturing activities, to some extent, are simpler because the item being costed is tangible. It may be a bottle of juice or a car. Even if it is a "one off," such as a bridge across a river, there is a distinguishable cost object. With service activities, it is sometimes more difficult to precisely define the outcome whether that is the cost of a haircut or a heart operation.

In Chapter 4, we defined the cost object as anything for which cost data is required. It is therefore possible to calculate the cost of any activity but there are some difficulties. In this section, we will consider separately the concept of cost in both the manufacturing and the service industries first.

Manufacturing Activities

In manufacturing, managers, at all levels, usually want to know the total cost of one manufactured unit, whether that is a tin of pet food or a specific one-off job. The main collection of data tends to be for that tangible asset. The usual focus is on the costs that can be traced directly to the product or products that are being manufactured by the enterprise. These costs comprise the following:

- Direct materials, which are those raw materials, parts, or sub-assemblies that are used in the production of the finished product. Note that this finished product may be sold to another organization as a part of a larger product. Automobile assembly is a good example.
- Direct wages, which represent the costs of those employees working directly on the manufacturing activity. Usually, supervisory costs would not be included as these tend to remain fixed irrespective of the activity level.

Service Activities

In the service sector, it can be more complex. Some of the aspects of service operations that should be taken into account when identifying the cost unit are:

- The cost of materials is usually insignificant and is often excluded from the cost classification.
- Direct labor can be highly significant. A method needs to be implemented that captures these costs.
- Allocation of overheads is far more complicated than in a manufacturing organization. An organization may decide that it is not worthwhile trying to allocate these costs to the specific service provided.

It may be difficult to define the cost unit and hypothetical ones must be generated. For example, a hotel may decide on calculating the cost unit as an occupied bed night; a transport company on a hybrid measure combining weight of cargo and distance mile.

In service organizations where an acceptable cost unit can be devised or where there are identifiable "jobs," absorption costing, which we explained in Chapter 4, can be applied for the allocation of overheads and the calculation of an allocation rate to arrive at the total cost. But given the differing characteristics of service organizations, new techniques, such as activity-based costing (ABC), aimed at allocating costs to various activities are attracting significant interest and application. We discussed the method in Chapter 4.

Whatever the nature of the industry, the main problem is selecting the method we should use to ensure that the appropriate amount of the indirect costs, that is, the overheads, are charged to the cost unit or activity. In most organizations, overhead costs are substantial and if we are going to price our activities correctly, we need to allocate an appropriate amount to the activity to determine its full cost.

One hurdle is the level of activity. Let us take a very simple example. A hairdressing salon has fixed overheads of $300 per day. These costs include the rental of the property and the wages of staff who are paid a fixed amount regardless of the number of customers. The variable costs, such as shampoo, are negligible. The owner from experience knows that, on average, a total of 30 clients will be attended on any one day. The average fixed cost per customer is therefore $10. If the client is charged $15, the profit for each customer should be $5 but this is based on the assumption that there are 30 customers.

If only 8 customers turn up, the profit will be:

Average daily overhead	$300
Receipts (8 × $15)	$120
Loss for day	$180

The above very simple example has demonstrated the importance of levels of activity. If we consider management decision making, a significant amount of the calculations is based on assumptions and estimates. There is no accounting method that reverse these errors but a good accounting system should be able to identify them so that managers can take appropriate action. For the hairdressing salon, there are two immediate options.

1. To charge each customer more assuming that the average number of customers will be eight. Unfortunately, this action may result in even fewer customers attending.

2. Reduce the cost of the hairdressing to the customer. The assumption is that this will increase trade but for the strategy to be effective, it must increase the daily volume of customers. This may lead to a need for larger premises and more staff to do the work. Both of these are fixed costs.

3. A further option is to pay the staff on the basis of customers they service each day. In other words, turn the fixed cost into a variable cost. However, the staff may be unwilling to work for an employer where the wages fluctuate on a daily basis.

Although we have chosen hairdressing as an example, the problem arises in many types of service companies. One solution that may be adopted is to guarantee staff a minimum wage but to pay additional wages if activity levels are high.

Selecting a Cost Strategy

In determining an organization's strategy, you are trying to achieve a future desired goal, but the information to assist you may be incomplete or uncertain. It is essential that the organization has some plans on what business targets it hopes to achieve and the resources it will need to do so. For some organizations, the immediate strategy may be the profit to be achieved in the next financial year or even the next month. Some enterprises may have a longer-term view involving takeovers, new product launches, and services offered.

Cost Leadership

Porter (1985) developed a Five Forces model, which can be helpful in determining the strategy of an organization. He proposed that the following competitive forces affect a company's profits:

1. The threat of new entrants into an industry or market served by a specific company
2. The bargaining power of suppliers
3. The bargaining power of the consumer

4. The threat of substitute products or services
5. The intensity of rivalry among existing companies

He argues that a successful company must develop a strategy that successfully recognizes these forces better than the strategy developed by its rivals. He suggested that a company must choose either of the following:

- Cost leadership, which involves offering a product or service at a lower price than its competitors.
- Competitor differentiation where the product or service is superior to its competitors and therefore customers are willing to pay more.

To determine which of these strategies to adopt, management need detailed and accurate financial information on their own costs. Without this information, no strategy can be developed.

Managerial Responsibilities

To implement the corporate strategy requires planning, making decisions, and controlling activities. A knowledge of the management accounting techniques that we addressed in Chapter 4 can help managers to successfully conduct their responsibilities. The main costing methods will assist managers in determining costs but the output of these methods must contribute to the organization's overall strategy. By comparing actual performance with predetermined performance, management can make assessments and conduct investigations to remedy deficiencies and to promote good practices.

An essential stage in the control loop is measuring actual performance against the plan. This is far more complex than it first appears as you are measuring the performance of people and how well they are carrying out their responsibilities. This requires a clear identification of the responsibility of a manager and the area for which the manager is responsible, which is usually a department or center but can be a specific activity.

Unfortunately, where managers have financial targets they are trying to achieve, this can lead to conflict or a disruption in services. If a manager attempts to reduce costs for their department, it may lead to poorer services to other departments in the production chain.

To avoid these conflicts, some organizations will make an internal charge to other parts of the organization for the services of a cost center. This does mean more record keeping and, possibly, interdepartmental arguments on the quality and cost of the service.

This dual nature of management accounting of providing information to meet the managers' needs and also assessing performance can lead to managers pursuing achievement of the performance measures at all costs, although this could be in conflict with what is required to achieve the overall organizational strategy.

For example, if the performance of a sales person is measured on the number of new customers obtained, there will be a tendency to concentrate on that and ignore maintaining a good relationship with existing customers. If employees are paid a bonus on the volume of work they achieve in a certain time, there may be a lack of attention to quality unless that is also measured in some way.

The problems of unwanted behaviors should not be overemphasized but managers need to be aware of them. Applying the methods we described in Chapter 4 is not only about generating financial information to support management decision making. It is about the activities of people and their endeavors to use the resources for which they have a responsibility to achieve an agreed strategy and financial success for the organization.

Because of these criticisms, several techniques have been developed, which aimed to be forward looking with an external focus. They cannot be claimed to be the sole preserve of the management account and some of them are designed to strengthen team building and the participation of every employee in the company. Two that have been used with some benefit are Activity Based Management and Total Quality Management.

Activity Based Management is closely related to Activity Based Costing and also concentrates on activities. Organizations undertake activities that consume resources. If these activities are analyzed and monitored, costs can be controlled at source. For instance, some activities can be enhanced and some may be eliminated. The activity is deemed value-added if the customer is willing to pay for it. Non-value adding activities should be eliminated as this would not affect the customer's perceived value of the product/service or impair the functioning and operation of the organization.

Total Quality Management is a philosophy rather than a technique. It is assumed that all processes, procedures, and practices can be improved. To bring about these improvements, TQM encourages employee empowerment. The first stage in implementing TQM is to identify customers and analyze their expectations. Measures are devised to make these expectations achievable in the production process. The measures can be both quantitative, for example, the time taken for a repair to be conducted or qualitative, for example, the image the customer yearns for in buying the product or service. Management and shop floor work together to attempt to bring about the required changes. One must be alert to the possibility that such an approach can lead to major internal disagreements.

Organizational Choices

Management accounting is used in hospitals, banks, universities, and manufacturing companies. Possibly in a simple format, it is used by plumbers, electricians, landscape gardeners, charities, and any other organization or individuals who need to know the financial consequences of the activities they undertake or the implications of those activities they plan to undertake.

These organizations have very different activities and may be pursuing very different strategies. Some will be manufacturers with substantial production facilities. Others will be merchandising companies that do no manufacturing but buy their goods and sell them at a profit. A very large sector of the economy is service organizations and, within this category, there is a great diversity ranging from financial institutions such as banks to hospitals, hotels, airlines, and others.

In profit-based organizations, there will be a strong relationship between the costs of activities and the market price for goods and services as this will determine profits. In non-profit organizations, the total amount of funds available for a period of time or a specific range of activities may be decided at the commencement of a financial period. Managers must ensure that the costs for which they are individually responsible fall within those limitations. Strategies will have financial boundaries set on them by external factors, such as donations and government grants.

There are no rules or regulations, which set out the form of management accounting that should be used by an organization. It is the responsibility of management to decide how internal information is collected and used. Such information must be useful as it can be expensive to collect. A number of methods have been developed over the years and we explain these in the next section.

Costing Methods

At the beginning of the 20th century, most accounting was financial accounting and, to a lesser extent, cost accounting. The latter was concerned with identifying the costs of products and processes within the company. It was internally orientated and focused on what had happened. In particular, the role of cost accounting was to establish the total cost incurred in production.

Although valuable new management accounting methods and techniques were being developed, some questioned whether the needs of management for information were met. There was a need for management accountants to provide information, which was of greatest value to the business. Accountants should change their perspective from a pure financial focus to a broader business perspective.

In this section, we consider management accounting techniques that focus on establishing the cost of a product or service and the relationship to profit. With all of these methods, organizations will usually amend the basic method to develop a system that produces the information that they find most useful.

Cost-Plus Pricing

One method of pricing products or services is to add on to the total costs (variable and fixed) a percentage amount to derive the market price. This is known as the cost-plus model. This method can only be used if the market is noncompetitive or only slightly competitive. This method ensures that you recover all your costs and make a profit. However, there are competitors and consumers with their own objectives. The competitors may be able to charge less for their products and the consumers will usually have a set price above which they will not go.

There is also the possibility that changes have occurred in the market environment where the company has operated or intends to do so. There may be competition from others who have adopted the strategy of cost leadership. Also, customers may place a different value on the product or service than the company has and will attempt to drive down the market price.

Despite these potential drawbacks, cost plus pricing remains a popular technique. The logic for its use is simple. To continue to exist, an organization must make a profit. Failure to do so will lead to bankruptcy. The solution to this dilemma may be found in the next costing method.

Target Costing

The alternative to the cost-plus model is to use target costing, also known as price-led costing. This involves setting of target costs for each product and each product related activity, starting with the design of the product and culminating with the sale of the product.

This technique ensures that the product is introduced to the market with a specific functionality, quality, and selling price, which can be produced at a life-cycle cost to generate an acceptable level of profitability (Cooper and Slagmulder 1997).

Target costing is not a complex technique although it requires a change in management thinking and philosophy in a company where the model has always been cost plus pricing. The possibilities of the value of target costing in even a small business have been identified by Tysiac (2017) who did the future planning of a family business.

In summary, the stages of Target Costing are described below:

- Calculate the target cost that satisfies the market price and the organization's target profit.
- Evaluate the types of actions that may be implemented in different departments or areas to bring actual costs in line with the target cost.

- Assess whether the reduction in costs in one area may lead to a consequential increase in costs in other areas.
- Set targets for each area in discussion with managers.
- Monitor the cost reductions to ensure that the actions implemented produce the required results.

It has been argued that the method of Target Costing is underused in the service sector, although its fairly simple to apply. A company using target costing collects market research data to ascertain the price customers are willing to pay given the product's functionality, quality and alternatives provided by competitors. The profit the company requires is deducted and the balance is the target cost. There are few real-life examples on how companies apply the method, but a case study illustration by Wakefield and Thamber (2019) illustrate the process in a service company.

Kaizen Costing

Kaizen costing may be used in manufacturing or the service sector. Kaizen encourages everyone in the company to continually reconsider how the task is undertaken and whether there is a better way of doing it. The technique concentrates on the production phase and on achieving continuous, incremental improvements over a period of time to reduce costs. The emphasis is on the process of production rather than the product. The principles can be used in the service sector. For example, a hospital may use the technique to reduce waiting times.

Companies establish their own procedures, but usually, there is a two-pronged approach with senior management and a work cell group. Management sets the cost reduction targets for the product. This may be done half yearly or even quarterly. The work cell group sets its targets. The two groups enter into negotiations to establish the policy. If there is an agreement between management and the work cell, the latter has considerable freedom in identifying ways to achieve these targets. Progress is monitored and if the cost reductions are not achieved, the reasons are sought. Costs are incrementally reduced for each period until the target profit is met.

It is suggested that the Kaizen approach has wider managerial benefits. It involves and empowers the workers, develops an organizational culture of learning, and creates a pride in work. There is the possible downside if the technique is continuously applied because employees may feel under constant pressure to improve their efforts.

Life Cycle Costing

Companies are increasingly concerned with the life cycle cost when they either purchase an item or manufacture it. Retirement and disposal costs have become increasingly important as environmental legislation compels companies to remedy damage that is caused by their operations.

If a company is implementing a new computerized system, there are additional costs apart from the initial cost of purchasing it. There will be the training costs of staff to operate the system, the possible costs of the supplier for maintenance, breakdowns, and upgrades. There is also likely to be the less quantifiable costs of the disruption caused during the implementation period. There may even be costs associated with running the old system and the new system until there is confidence in its efficiency. Finally, there may be costs associated with the abandonment or dismantling of the system, for example, a nuclear power plant.

Life cycle costing is designed to determine the total of all the costs of a product, service, or asset over a defined period of time. The costs include acquisition, installation, operation, production, maintenance, refurbishment, and disposal. The technique is future orientated and compels managers to examine the long-term financial implications of the strategic decisions they are making. It also encourages managers to examine and question the costs incurred at every significant stage in the entire life of the product. One study by Knauer and Möslang (2018) has found that companies reported that the greatest benefit of LCC is related to the identification of cost drivers. This is critical knowledge if a business is to be managed successfully.

Managing the Business

This chapter has concentrated on management accounting techniques. Although it is essential that a company concentrates on cost management, this comes under the general heading of managing the business and all that it entails. The application of a costing method in a business is essential to its proper management. In this section, we explain two techniques that are frequently used, Activity Based Management and Total Quality Management.

Activity Based Management

ABM is a logical follow on for companies using Activity Based Costing. The objective is maximizing value-added activities whilst eliminating or minimizing non-value-added activities. These activities are defined by the consumers' reactions. In applying ABM, it is intended that organizational efficiency will be improved with lowering costs and, hopefully, increasing output. There are a number of ways that costs can be reduced such as increasing efficiency and establishing performance measures.

The activities that are pursued by a company must necessarily consume resources. By controlling activities at their source, action can be taken to reduce costs. Caution must be used because the consumer of the activity will also have an opinion on how much they should pay for the product or service. If the customer is willing to pay, these are known as value added activities. If the customer's perceived value of the product or service is not impaired, the particular activity can be reduced or stopped.

In a manufacturing environment, management may look at the costs incurred in the storage and internal transport of raw materials, work in process, and finished goods. It may adopt a system such as "Just-In-Time" deliveries, which can reduce some of these internal costs. In a service environment, customers may spend time waiting, which may impact negatively on their impressions of the company. Many of us do not enjoy waiting in a queue and providing suitable "waiting room" can be costly. By improving service, a company may lead to improved customer satisfaction and lower costs.

Total Quality Management (TQM)

Although not specifically an accounting method, the technique may enhance corporate financial performance. It assumes that all the employees of the organization are responsible for the quality of products and processes with the clear objective of meeting or exceeding customer expectations.

The technique is based on the premise that there can be continuous improvement of all the processes, procedures, and practices. Employees are encouraged and sometimes financially rewarded for making suggestions that will reduce costs and/or improve the product or service. There is plenty of guidance on implementing and operating TQM. Powell (1995) has constructed a list of the following 12 factors for a successful TQM.

1. **Committed leadership:** a near-evangelical, unwavering, long-term commitment by top managers to the philosophy, usually under a term similar to Total Quality Management, Continuous Improvement (CI), or Quality Improvement (QI).
2. **Adoption and communication of TQM:** using tools like the mission statement, and themes or slogans.
3. **Closer customer relationships:** determining both internal and external customers' requirements, then meeting those requirements no matter what it takes.
4. **Closer supplier relationships:** working closely and cooperatively with suppliers and ensuring they provide inputs that conform to customers' end-use requirements.
5. **Benchmarking:** researching and observing best competitive practices.
6. **Increased training:** usually includes TQM principles, team skills, and problem-solving.
7. **Open organization:** lean staff, empowered work teams, open horizontal communications, and a relaxation of traditional hierarchy.
8. **Employee empowerment:** increased employee involvement in design and planning, and greater autonomy in decision making.
9. **Zero-defects mentality:** a system in place to spot defects as they occur, rather than through inspection and rework.
10. **Flexible manufacturing:** (applicable only to manufacturers) can include just-in-time inventory, cellular manufacturing, design for manufacturability (DFM), statistical process control (SPC), and design of experiments (DQE).

11. **Process improvement:** reduced waste and cycle times in all the areas through cross departmental process analysis.

12. **Measurement:** goal-orientation and zeal for data, with constant performance measurement, often using statistical methods.

TQM may bring financial and other types of improvement but it is not necessarily appropriate for every company. Dayton (2003) has suggested that lack of understanding and clarity in applying TQM led to negative publicity and an environment that weakened and eroded the foundations of TQM.

Conclusions

The analysis of the financial performance of an organization reflects the nature of the management. In this chapter, we have concentrated on explaining how the costing or management accounting practices we discussed in Chapter 4 can be applied to improve the financial performance of an organization. The first stage for any organization is establishing objectives and measuring your progress in achieving them. A substantial part of any plan will be the costs that have to be incurred in their operations. We consider that an organization must have a business plan, expressed in financial terms, and some form of record keeping to measure regularly their success, or otherwise, in meeting the plan.

A business plan can be set by even a small organization. For larger companies, there is the need to look closely at the costs that it incurs in its activities. We have described the different costing aspects in manufacturing and service industries and how to select a cost strategy. There are a number of costing methods and the one an organization selects depends on its size and type of industry. We emphasize that the organization should be automatically changed to meet the technique. An organization has its own culture, and strengths and weaknesses. The technique is molded to meet the needs of the business.

We have completed the chapter by describing two main financial approaches that have been proposed for managing a business. These are activity-based management and total quality management. With both of these, we have focused on the accounting dimension, but we appreciate fully that management of any business has other important dimensions.

Action Plan

Identify the company in which you are interested and determine the type of operations it does whether servicing or manufacturing or a combination of both.

- Look for similar companies to act as comparisons
- Try to find data for that particular industry.
- Try to determine which costs are fixed or variable.
- Ascertain what the company methods are.
- Compare the methods the company uses with what you have read in these chapters.

CHAPTER 6

Accounting and Business Developments

About This Chapter

The collection and analysis of corporate data is an expanding field. In the previous chapters, we have focused on the financial data of companies that is readily available in reports and websites, and also on the accounting data and methods used within organizations.

The financial data gives only one aspect of an organization's operations. In recent years, there has been legislation and encouragements to provide a more comprehensive analysis. Although you can analyze an organization's available financial data, there are other important aspects to investigate. Important questions such as "Can the organization obtain the basic resources to stay in business?" and "Are its activities harmful to the environment?" may be more important than "What was the profit?"

In this chapter, we take a broader view of an organization's activities than only the financial performance. First, we consider how the amount of information issued by companies has expanded through the issue of a Management Discussion and Analysis contained in the annual report. We also consider the masses of data that is available to the company and how it may use data analytics to improve its decision making.

The second section of this chapter explains the use of Key Performance Indicators (KPIs). This subject is of increasing interest as it explains how companies can measure their performance and the information that is made available publicly. If you are investigating the specific performance of an organization, KPIs can be of considerable interest.

The last two sections of the chapter address the possible expansion of information made available to shareholders and others interested in the conduct of a business. Section 3 is concerned with sustainability accounting. The 2007/8 economic crisis revealed that financial reporting by itself does not provide sufficient information on short-term and long-term business performance. Also, the financial data does not address other aspects of company activities and their impact on such topics such as global warning. Our final section explains the concept of integrated financial reporting, which helps to draw the various issues together.

Information Expansion

Over the years, the amount of information that a company listed on a stock exchange makes available has expanded considerably. Some of this is required by legislation but a substantial amount is voluntarily provided by companies. To obtain the information that has been made publicly available, you can either contact the company or enter the electronic filing system if the company is listed on a stock exchange.

In the United States, the Securities and Exchange Commission states on its website that its role is to protect investors, promote fairness in the securities markets, and shares information about companies and investment professionals to help investors make informed decisions and invest with confidence. Their website is https://sec.gov/ If the company you are interested in is registered in the UK, you need to enter the website https://gov.uk/government/organisations/companies-house In Canada, the System for Electronic Document Analysis and Retrieval (SEDAR) is an electronic filing system for the disclosure documents of public companies and investment funds across Canada, https://www.sedar.com/

In addition to registering their financial statements with the appropriate authorities, companies have their own websites that contain substantial amounts of information and will also issue press releases. The following is an example from a Canadian company issued on May 1, 2019.

> Loblaw Companies Limited (TSX: L) ("Loblaw" or the "Company") today announced its unaudited financial results for the first quarter ended March 23, 2019. The Company's 2019 First Quarter Report to Shareholders will be available in the Investors section of the Company's website at loblaw.ca and will be filed with SEDAR and available at sedar.com

Loblaw, as with most other companies, not only complies with the regulations concerning disclosure of information, but also provides information that it considers best reflects its financial performance. These are usually known as non-GAAP measures. GAAP stands for Generally Accepted Accounting Principles. In providing this additional information, Loblaw, as with many companies, explains fully its rationale as shown in the following News Release that detailed its financial performance in the first quarter of 2019.

Non-GAAP Financial Measures

The Company uses non-GAAP financial measures as they believe these measures provide useful information to both management and investors in measuring the financial performance and financial condition of the Company. Reconciliations of the non-GAAP financial measures contained in this News Release are reconciled to GAAP financial measures in the section below.

Management uses these and other non-GAAP financial measures to exclude the impact of certain expenses and income that must be recognized under GAAP when analyzing underlying consolidated and segment operating performance, as the excluded items are not necessarily reflective of the Company's underlying operating performance and make comparisons of underlying financial performance between periods difficult. The Company excludes additional items if it believes doing so would result in a more effective analysis of underlying operating performance.

The exclusion of certain items does not imply that they are non-recurring. These measures do not have a standardized meaning prescribed by GAAP, and therefore, they may not be comparable to similarly titled measures presented by other publicly traded companies and should not be construed as an alternative to other financial measures determined in accordance with GAAP.

For a more complete description of the Company's non-GAAP financial measures and financial metrics, please refer to Section 12 "Non-GAAP Financial Measures" of the Company's 2019 First Quarter Report to Shareholders.

Source: Press Release Loblaw Reports 2019 First Quarter Results and a 6.8% Increase to Quarterly Common Share

As with all the additional information provided by companies, whether in their own printed documents, press releases, or some other method, the question arises as to which one should you believe. The situation is compounded by the fact that the United States has not adopted the accounting regulations established by the International Accounting Standards Board (Hussey and Ong 2018).

A company, therefore, following International Accounting Standards, can publish financial results that may be different from those if it had followed the U.S. GAAP. We would also add that any figure of profit a company issues in accordance with the accounting regulations in a country, is likely to be different from the amount that the tax authorities will calculate because they have their own regulations.

We do not wish to exaggerate these differences, but to emphasize that the growth in the amount of information, financial and otherwise, issued by companies can make any examination of their financial results difficult especially where you are trying to compare organizations in different countries. The solution is to be consistent in the information you are choosing to use and to be aware of possible differences in accounting practices.

Management Discussion and Analysis

In addition to the financial statements, a company may also include in its annual report and accounts, information that can provide a much deeper insight into a company's operations. In the United States, companies listed on the Stock Exchange are required to issue a Management Discussion and Analysis Statement.

If you are examining the annual financial reports of companies in other countries, there may not be a Management Discussion and Analysis Statement as a section of the annual report. However, you may find statements that provide the same types of information and these are usually titled as "Strategic Report," "Operating and Financial Review," or similar. Even if there are no sections labeled, you may find the types of information we discuss in this chapter contained in the Director's Report in the company's annual report and accounts.

If we take the U.S. MD&A as our model, the types of information you will find are as follows:

1. Any trends, events, commitments, demands, or uncertainties that are likely to result in material changes in the liquidity of the company or its capital resources.
2. Any unusual events, transactions and economic changes that have affected income from continuing operations. For example, if there has been a significant change in net revenue compared to previous periods, the company should explain the degree to which the increase is due to a price increase, introduction of a new product or service, or to some other factor.
3. A full explanation of the company's accounting policies. This helps investors to understand the methods the company used to construct its financial statement.

An example of the MD&A is the following extract from the Form 10-K submitted by Apple to the SEC. It is a lengthy report and pages 22–34 focus on the MD&A. We show below a small extract that explains the company's gross margin.

Gross margin for 2018, 2017 and 2016 was as follows (dollars in millions):

	2018	2017	2016
Net sales	$265,595	$229,234	$215,639
Cost of sales	163,756	141,048	131,376
Gross margin	$101,839	$88,186	$84,263
Gross margin percentage	38.3%	38.5%	39.1%

Gross margin increased in 2018 compared to 2017 due primarily to a favorable shift in mix of iPhones with higher average selling prices and higher Services net sales, partially offset by higher product cost structures. Gross margin percentage decreased year over-year due

> primarily to higher product cost structures, partially offset by higher Services net sales. The strength in foreign currencies relative to the U.S. dollar had a favorable impact on gross margin and gross margin percentage during 2018.

Data Analytics

A complete explanation of Data Analytics, sometimes referred to as Big Data, is outside the scope of this book. It is important, however, to explain its potential impact on business decision making and corporate reporting and the impact on you in your investigations. The technique undoubtedly can assist decision making but mastering its application does require some specialized knowledge.

Data Analytics has been defined as "the process of evaluating data with the purpose of drawing conclusions to address business questions" (Richardson, Terrell, and Teeter 2019). The term Big Data is sometimes used and this can be regarded as thousands of observations on a subject from many sources. For example, the use of a money-off coupon to purchase a product identifies the measure of consumer interest. It may also reveal consumers' preferences and data on their background.

Big data is continually being collected and there is likely to be masses of data collected from many sources, which is original data and has not been interpreted in any way. Usually, the collection of the data is an automatic process but, as it is coming from its original source, it is unlikely to be structured or organized in any particular format. This results in difficulties in the analysis of the data and drawing conclusions to aid business decision making.

To overcome these difficulties in analysis, Data Analytics uses specialized software tools for analyzing large sets of data to identify patterns and to determine those that are most relevant for making business decisions. To start the process of analysis, Isson and Harriott (2013) have constructed a model named the IMPACT cycle. Its stages are:

> Identify the issue for which you need information to make a decision. In other words, you need to define a question to which you require an answer. Examples are determining the price for a

product or service, or identifying waste and fraud occurring in the work place.

Master the data that is relevant to answering the question. This means ascertaining the data needed to answer your question and finding whether it is collectable and reliable.

Perform test plan that involves determining whether an analysis of the data may provide the answer you seek.

Address and refine the results so that opinions can be made on the outcomes.

Communicate insights to others involved in decision making.

Track the outcomes on a regular basis

Various claims are made concerning the value of Data Analytics and an increasing number of organizations are using Big Data, although there is little information in the public domain on how it is being used and its successes in contributing to business performance. It is probable that as Data Analytics and Big Data become more widely used, it will come under the responsibility of the accounting function in an organization and will influence the types of financial information provided by companies and the nature of the information used in the management accounting system.

In earlier chapters, we have explained that both management accounting information and financial reporting are subject to a certain level of estimates and predictions. Data Analytics may ensure that the information in the financial statements will contain more reliable information. For example, at the end of a financial period, a manufacturing company is likely to have goods ready for sale and items part completed. Data Analytics should provide us with more accurate information on their value than we have at present. Most companies have money owed to them. Data Analytics should be able to give us information on how much will probably be received and the ratio of bad debts.

Although Data Analytics offers improvement in the accuracy of the information generated by organizations, both for internal use and external distribution, it is the responsibility of the users of data to assess the information and determine what action should be taken. Organizations will continue to issue the financial statements we described in Chapter 2 and you can analyze them using the techniques we discussed in Chapter 3. Managers in the manufacturing and services sector will continue to receive financial information regularly and apply the techniques and strategies we have discussed in Chapters 4 and 5. The difference will be that the information may be more reliable and provide a more complete picture of corporate activities.

Key Performance Indicators

Key performance indicators are an important component of the disclosures used to describe and explain information that reveals a company's progress in achieving its strategy. Such measures may be named KPIs but some companies and commentators refer to them as Additional (or Alternative) Performance Measures "APMs."

Although our following explanation of KPIs is directed at those who are outside of a particular organization in which they are interested, performance indicators enable decision makers to take action. They can give an early signal of increasing risk exposure giving management and the board significant insight into how effectively the organization manages risks and resolves performance issues.

Whether you are an insider of an organization or examining an external document you need to understand each KPI that is used. To achieve this position, you should be able to find answers to the following:

- The definition and calculation method
- The purpose or objective in calculating the ratio
- The source of underlying data
- Any significant assumptions made
- Any changes in the calculation method used compared to previous financial years

KPIs are not necessarily financial in nature and could refer to labor turnover, wastage of raw materials, returned goods, customer complaints, and other aspects of the organization. As such, they may be good indicators of an organization's future financial prospects and progress in managing risks and opportunities.

Mostly, the KPIs provided by an organization are closely related to the industry in which a company operates. The literature is replete with suggestions of the most appropriate KPIs and examples of KPIs suitable for specific types of industry. An indication (PricewaterhouseCooper 2007) of the types of KPIs that are appropriate for three different industries is shown in the following Table 6.1.

Table 6.1 KPIs in different industries

Banking	Petroleum	Retail
Customer retention	Capital expenditure	Capital expenditure
Customer penetration	Exploration success rate	Store portfolio changes
Asset quality	Refinery utilization	Expected return on new stores
Capital adequacy	Refinery capacity	Customer satisfaction
Assets under management	Volume of proven and probable reserves	Same store/like-for-like sales
Loan loss	Reserve replacement costs	Sales per square foot/meter

There are also KPIs for different issues. In 2012, The Department for Environment Food and Rural Affairs (Defra) commenced an informal consultation to seek views on revised guidance for how the UK organizations should measure and report on their environmental impacts. This guidance was intended to replace the current guidance, which was published in 2006.

The guidance sets out general principles for how to measure and report on environmental key performance indicators (KPIs). It suggests a structured means for reporting those indicators and covers the following five areas:

1. Air pollution and other emissions
2. Water
3. Biodiversity/ecosystem services
4. Materials
5. Waste

If you have an interest in understanding fully an organization's activities, KPIs and APMs can provide extremely useful information. They usually consist of data that is not easily extracted from the audited financial statements. However, the unsophisticated user may not be aware that some measures are recalculations of the profit as shown on the legally compliant financial statements. They are essentially alternative performance measures. The user may also not realize that some measures, as well as not being financial but quantitative, have not been audited. Companies provide this information, presumably, because they consider that the profit calculation under accounting standards does not give a complete picture of management's method of measuring financial performance. That may be the case but we encourage you to use caution in interpreting the data.

Key performance indicators are an important component of the disclosures used to describe and explain an organization's progress in achieving its strategy. We would emphasize that KPIs provide additional information to that found in the financial section of the annual report and accounts. However, you need to assess the reliability of the KPIs that are provided and the following list offers guidelines.

1. Why is the organization voluntarily providing this information? If it is legally required and are the regulations being met?
2. How is the KPI defined, and what is its purpose?
3. How reliable is the source of the original data?
4. What is the definition of the KPI and how is it calculated?
5. If the KPI is compared to previous years, is the basis of the calculations the same?

Companies usually provide a full explanation of their KPIs and how they are calculated. The following extract is taken from Diageo Annual Report 2019 p. 12:

Definition
Sales growth after deducting excise duties, excluding the impact of exchange rate movements, acquisitions and disposals.

Why we measure
This measure reflects our performance as the result of the choices made in terms of category and market participation, and Diageo's ability to build brand equity, increase prices and grow market share.

Performance
Organic net sales grew 6.1%, driven by 2.3% volume growth and 3.8% positive price/mix. Growth was broad based with all regions delivering net sales growth.

KPIs and APMs supply useful information. They usually provide data that is not easily extracted from the audited financial statements. However, the unsophisticated user may not be aware that some measures are recalculations of the profit as shown on the IFRS compliant financial statements. They are essentially alternative performance measures. The user may also not realize that some measures, as well as not being financial but quantitative, have not been audited. Although most companies issue KPIs that are reliable, you should be aware of the following possible weaknesses

- Bias in the calculations
- Inconsistency in the calculations from year to year
- Inaccurate classification of items
- Insufficient information on the basis for the calculations
- No reconciliation with the audited profit figure
- Inadequate definition of terms

Key performance indicators help managers to analyze and interpret how well their organizations function. Choosing just a few operational data points to include in a review reduces complexity. Successful managers identify their informational needs and determine what data to use as business performance indicators. By examining performance levels, managers can see where problems lie and develop improvement strategies. Additionally, company executives review KPI reports to monitor the overall business and make strategic management decisions. In some cases,

KPI reports produced as part of annual financial statements also allow companies to demonstrate compliance with reporting regulations.

Although you can calculate the financial ratios for many types of organizations, there are also non-profit organizations of very different types that use, and frequently publish, interesting ratios. In Ontario, Canada, KPIs have been in use since 1998 to measure the performance of higher education institutions in the province. All post-secondary schools collect and report performance data in five areas. It may be that in your own organization you have been using different types of performance indicators for several years without realizing that large companies are now publishing such data.

It is the decision of the company to determine which KPIs it should report. Many choose financial indicators. Not surprisingly, many companies select KPIs that are specific to the industry in which they operate although some will match their disclosures to other companies. The Securities Exchange Commission (SEC) has issued guidance, which became effective February 25, 2020. It addresses the disclosure of key performance indicators and metrics in Management's Discussion and Analysis of Financial Condition and Results of Operations (MD&A). While this guidance may not have been an area of significant focus for many companies, it suggests that KPIs may become of greater importance in the future.

Sustainability Accounting

If you are the owner or the employee of a small company, sustainability accounting may not be on your list of priorities. However, if you have dealings with larger companies and wish to understand what is happening, you will find it useful to refer to their website. Aspects of sustainability accounting can be found under a number of different names. For example, social and environmental accounting, corporate social reporting, corporate social responsibility reporting, or non-financial reporting.

The term sustainability accounting is now the most frequently used. It is related to the financial statements but connects the companies' strategies from a *sustainable* framework. It does this by disclosing information on the three levels that are environment, economic, and social. As you can imagine, there is some difficulty in combining these three categories into a format that is easily understood.

The Sustainability Accounting Standards Boards (SASB) is the authority on corporate disclosures and was established in 2011. It issues standards and its website contains useful information (https://sasb.org). It states that it is concerned with the following activities.

Financially Material: SASB's mission is to help businesses around the world identify, manage and report on the sustainability topics that matter most to their investors.

Market Informed: SASB standards are developed based on extensive feedback from companies, investors, and other market participants as part of a transparent, publicly-documented process.

Industry Specific: SASB standards differ by industry, enabling investors and companies to compare performance from company to company within an industry.

The SASB Foundation operates in a governance structure similar to the structure adopted by other internationally recognized bodies that set standards for disclosure of financial and other types of corporate information. The SASB has a board of directors responsible for the strategy, finances, and operations of the entire organization. There is also a standard-setting board that develops, issues, and maintains the SASB standards. The SASB Foundation receives no government financing and is not affiliated with any governmental body.

In 2018, the SASB published a complete set of 77 industry standards. These identify the set of financially material sustainability topics and their associated metrics for the typical company in an industry. The standards are intended to assist organizations in identifying and communicating opportunities for sustaining long-term value creation. The standards are available for download on the SASB website at https://www.sasb.org/

Companies adopt their own approach to sustainability account and the information they provide. We have extracted some details of a sustainability report by Estée Lauder. The full report has 89 pages.

This report provides a review of The Estée Lauder Companies' citizenship and sustainability activities and performance since our last progress report, which was published in June 2019. The content covers our priority focus areas. Unless otherwise noted, this report covers activities during our fiscal 2019 (July 1, 2018 to June 30, 2019) and includes data for facilities we own and operate.

This report has been prepared in accordance with the standards outlined by the Global Reporting Initiative (GRI): Core option.

Our citizenship and sustainability goals are in focus areas where we believe we have an opportunity to positively impact the environment and society. We announced many of these goals in March, 2019. Below is our progress against the goals as of June 30, 2019.

FOCUS AREA	GOAL 1	FISCAL 2019 PROGRESS
ENERGY AND EMISSIONS	By 2020, we will achieve Net Zero carbon emissions and RE100.	We are on track to achieve Net Zero carbon emissions and RE100 by 2020. Net Zero: 39% progress toward goal RE100 Progress: 66% of electricity sourced from renewable sources
	By 2020, we will build upon our Net Zero carbon emissions commitment and set a science-based target (SBT) covering Scopes 1, 2 and 3.	We have committed to setting a science-based target covering our Scope 1, 2 and 3 emissions. For more information, *please visit the Science Based Targets website.*
WASTE	By 2020, we will achieve zero industrial waste-to-landfill for all global manufacturing and distribution sites. We expanded this goal in fiscal 2017 to include all global distribution and innovation sites.	100% of global manufacturing sites sent zero industrial waste to landfill. 85% of global distribution sites sent zero industrial waste to landfill. 60% of global innovation sites sent zero industrial waste to landfill.

EMPLOYEE SAFETY	We will drive safety to continue decreasing the total incident rate 3 to ensure continued world class–leading levels, with a goal of 0.15 by 2025.	Our Total Incident Rate was 0.25.

Integrated Financial Reporting

No longer is it only management and investors that are interested in the activities of an organization. Others such as suppliers, customers, and many other groups wish to know how an organization operates. Also, the general public is becoming more interested in the impact of an organization's activities. As we saw in the previous section, sustainability accounting and the impact of an organization on such matters as waste, pollution, natural resource usage, and climate change is now high on the list of disclosure of an organization's activities. The expansion in the amount of information disclosed can be confusing. The links between the different elements need to be made clear and integrated financial reporting has emerged as a possible solution.

The International Integrated Reporting Council (IIRC) was formed in 2010 having previously been named the International Financial Reporting Committee. Their current website (https://integratedreporting.org/) contains explanations of their aims and their suggestions for good practices. The emphasis is on businesses' value creation and its aim is to be the next step in the evolution of corporate reporting. It states its mission is to create the globally accepted International IR Framework that elicits from organizations information about their strategy, governance, performance and prospects in a clear, concise, and comparable format. The Integrated Report explains an organization's strategy, governance, performance, and prospects, in the context of its external environment.

The <IR> Framework takes a principles-based approach that ensures it is usable by organizations of any size and in any sector. It also sets out a number of requirements that are to be applied before an integrated report can be said to be in accordance with the <IR> Framework.

The IIRC is very active and is supported by many national standards setting organizations. However, from the research they have conducted,

Slack and Cambell (2019) concluded that although there is some use of and familiarity with <IR>, it appears to be limited and that there is little evidence of either use of or demand for <IR> among many mainstream fund managers or sell-side analysts.

At this stage, it is difficult to measure the extent of information provided by companies and its use by recipients of Integrated Reports. A guide to the stage of development in the United States can be found on the following website: https://iruscommunity.org/directory-united-states-integrated-reports. A review of the progress of Integrated Reporting can be found on https://drcaroladams.net/evidence-of-the-take-up-of-integrated-reporting/. Needless to say, all the large firms of accountants have a substantial amount of information on the subject on their websites.

Conclusions

In this chapter, we have adopted a broader view of an organization's activities. The focus has not been on the financial reports published by companies but a wide range of information that links corporate activities more closely to society as a whole. The range of information that larger companies make public has expanded significantly.

Key Performance Indicators are based on the financial statements but give a different view of an organization's achievements. When we consider the remaining two sections in this chapter, Sustainability Accounting and Integrated Financial Reporting, we are moving away from the focus on the financial achievements. We are moving toward a view of the organization's impact on society.

This expansion in available information should be kept in perspective. If you are interested in a small, local organization, much of the information we have discussed in this chapter will not be available. It is the large companies listed on a stock exchange that issue information on sustainability and that integrate their financial reports. Such information is of interest not only to investors but also many others who are interested in the impact on the way we live and address such issues as global warming, waste disposal, and protecting natural resources.

We cannot envisage any reduction in the amount of information distributed by large companies. It is you, the user, who must decide the information you want and how you are going to use it. In this book, we have attempted to assist you in that process.

Action Plan

Identify a large company in which you may have an interest. You may work for it, use its products, or wish to know more about its activities. We suggest you follow these stages of investigation:

1. Calculate those financial ratios, described in Chapter 2, in which you are most interested. You need to determine any trends by calculating ratios for five years.
2. Investigate the reasons for any significant movements in the trend.
3. If the company report contains KPIs, compare these with your own calculations.
4. Where the company has adopted sustainability accounting, determine whether you agree with their comments and does it correspond with the financial ratios you have.

As a last stage, compare your views with the opinions in the financial newspapers and on the various websites that analyze corporate performance. If they differ significantly from your opinion, you may become a millionaire or a pauper.

References

Alali, F., and S. Wang. November 2017. "Characteristics of Financial Restatements and Frauds. An Analysis of Corporate Reporting Quality from 2000–2014." *CPA Journal*, pp. 32–41.

Amiram, D., Z. Bozanic, J.D. Cox, Q, Dupont, J.M. Karpoff, and R. Sloan. January 23, 2018. "Financial Reporting Fraud and Other Forms of Misconduct: A Multidisciplinary Review of the Literature." *Review of Accounting Studies*, pp. 732–83. https://doi.org/10.1007/s11142-017-9435-x

Boyns, T., and J.R. Edwards. 2013. *A History of Management Accounting*. New York and London: Routledge.

Burks, J.J. 2015. "Accounting Errors in Nonprofit Organizations." *Accounting Horizons. American Accounting Association* 29, no. 2, pp. 341–61. doi: 10.2308/acch-51017

Carmichael, D.R. March 2020. "Financial Statement Fraud by External Parties." *CPA Journal*, pp. 28–34.

Cashwell, K., P. Copley, and M. Dugan. May 2019. Using Ratio Analysis to Manage Not-for-Profit Organizations. *CPA Journal*, pp. 52–57.

Cooper, R., and R. Slagmulder, 1997. *Target Costing and Value Engineering*. Portland, OR: Productivity Press.

Daniels, R.B., M. Braswell, and J.D. Beeler. December 2010. "Accounting and Financial Reporting by a Late 18th Century American Charity." *Accounting Historians Journal* 37, no. 2, pp. 39–65.

Dayton, N.A. 2003. "The Demise of Total Quality Management." *TQM Magazine* 15, no. 6, 391–96. doi:10.1108/09544780310502723

Elkington, J. 1997. *Cannibals with Forks: The Triple Bottom Line of 21st Century Business*. Oxford, UK: Capstone Publishing.

Fitzsimons, A.P., I.N. McCarthy, and B.R Silliman. 2018. "FASB Issues New Guidance to Improve Financial Reporting for Not-for-Profit Organizations." *Review of Business: Interdisciplinary Journal on Risk and Society* 38, no. 1, pp. 36–46.

Frank, W.G. 1979. "An Emperical Analysis of International Accounting Principles." *Journal of Accounting Research* 17, no. 2, pp. 593–605.

Galbraith, K. 2009. *The Great Crash 1929*, Reprint ed. New York, NY: Mariner Books.

Gowthorpe, C., and G. Flynn. August 1997. "Reporting on the Web: The State of the Art." *Accountancy*.

Hussey, R. 2000. "Consuming Information: The Need for Safety Regulations." *Knowledge and Process Management* 7, no. 3, 143–50. doi:10.1002/1099-1441(200007/09)7:3<143::AID-KPM84>3.0.CO;2-S

Hussey, R., and A. Ong. 2018. *Pick a Number: The U.S. and International Accounting*, 2nd ed. Business Expert Press.

Isson, J.P., and J.P. Harriott. 2013. *Win with Advanced Business Analytics: Creating Business Value from Your Data*. Wiley.

Johnston, R., and R. Petacchi. Summer 2017. "Regulatory Oversight of Financial Reporting: Securities and Exchange Commission Comment Letters." *Contemporary Accounting Research* 34, no. 2, 1128–55. © CAAA doi:10.1111/1911-3846.12297

Kaplan, R.S., and W. Bruns. 1987. *Accounting and Management: A Field Study Perspective*. Boston, MA: Harvard Business School Press.

Kaplan, R.S., and S.R. Anderson. November 2004. "Time-Driven Activity-Based Costing." *Harvard Business Review* 82, no. 11, pp. 66–69.

Khokhar, A.R. March-June 2019. "Working Capital Investment. A Comparative Study Canada v United States." *Multinational Finance Journal* 23, nos. 1/2, pp. 65–102, 38.

Khoufia, W., and D. Khrifech. 2018. "Country-Specific Characteristics Influencing Websites Based Information Disclosure." *Accounting and Management Information Systems* 17, no. 3, 374–405. doi:10.24818/jamis.2018.03004

Lin, S., D. Martinez, C. Wang, and Y. Yang. 2018. "Is Other Comprehensive Income Reported in the Income Statement More Value Relevant? The Role of Financial Statement Presentation." *Journal of Accounting, Auditing & Finance* 33, no. 4, 624–46. doi:10.1177/0148558X16670779

Linnane, C., F. McKenna, and K. Marriner. November 26, 2019. "The SEC may be Cracking Down on Companies that Adjusr Revenue." *Marketwatch*.

Mechelli, A., and R. Cimini. 2014. "Is Comprehensive Income Value Relevant and Does Location Matter? A European Study." *Accounting in Europe* 11, no. 1, pp. 59–87. doi:10.1080/17449480.2014.890777

Meric, G., B. Guner, S. Chung, and I. Meric. 2019. "A Comparison of Buiness Management Cgaracteristics in U. S., German and Japanese Manufacturing Corrporations." *Studies in Business and Economics* 14, no. 1, 141–53. doi:10.2478/sbe-2019-0011

Mishra, L., and P.K. Haldar. April 2019. "Narrative Disclosures in Corporate Annual Report: A Critical Review of Literature." *IUP Journal of Accounting Research & Audit Practices* 18, no. 2, pp. 7–19, 13p.

Mueller, G.G. 1967. *International Accounting*. New York: NY, Macmillan.

Nair, R.D., and W.G. Frank. July 1980. "The Impact of Disclosure and Measurement Practices on International Accounting Classifications." *Accounting Review* 55, no. 3, pp. 426–50.

Nel, G., and L. Esterhuyse. Spring 2019. "Corporate Websites as Stakeholder Communication Channel. A Comparison of JSE-Listed Companies Websites Over Time." *Journal of Global Business and Technology* 15, no. 1, pp. 34–46.

Nobes, C.W. Spring 1983. "A Judgemental International Classification of Financial Reporting Practices." *Journal of Business Finance and Accounting* 10, no. 1, pp. 1–19.

Parks, L. 2019. "Our Enduring Legacy: The History of IMA." *Strategic Finance* 100, no. 12, pp. 28–31.

Parker, R.H., and B.S. Yarney. 1994. *Accounting History*. Oxford. UK: Oxford University Press.

Pendley, J.A., and A. Rai. 2009. "Internet Financial Reporting: An Examination of Current Practice." *International Journal of Disclosure and Governance* 6, no. 2, pp. 89–105.

Porter, M.R. 1985. *Competitive Advantage*. New York, NY: Free Press.

Powell, T.C. 1995. "Total Quality Management as Competitive Advantage: A Review and Empirical Study." *Strategic Management Journal* 16, no. 1, pp. 15–37.

Previts, G.J., and B.D. Marino. 1998. *A History of Accountancy in the United States: The Cultural Significance of Accounting*. Athens, OH: Ohio State University Press.

Pticar, S. 2016. *Financing as One of the Key Success Factors of Small and Medium-Sized Enterprises*, 1–12. De Gruyter Open DOI: 10.1515/cks-2016-0010

Richardson, V.J., K. Terrell, and R. Teeter. 2019. *Data Analytics for Accounting*. McGraw. Hill.

Robson, L.W. 1943. "The Trend Towards Uniformity in Costing Methods in Industry." *Accountant* 109, no. 3578, pp. 6–10.

Sangster, A., and G. Scataglinibelghitar. 2010. "Luca Pacioli: The Father of Accounting Education." *Accounting Education* 19, no. 4, pp. 423–28.

Schutte, J., and J.R. Duncan. August 2019. "The Statement of Cash Flows Turns 30. Common Reporting Deficiencies and Recent Changes." *The CPA Journal*, pp. 6–10.

Sedki, S.S., G.A. Posada, and K.A. Pruske. August 2018. "Differences Between U.S. GAAP and IFRS in Accounting for Goodwill Impairment and Inventory: Tax Treatment Under the Internal Revenue Code." *Journal of Accounting & Finance* (2158–3625) 18, no. 4, 23–29, 7. doi: 10.33423/jaf.v18i4.421

Slack, R., and D. Cambell. 2016. *Meeting Users' Information Needs: The Use and Usefulness of Integrated Reporting*. Association of Certified Chartered Accountants.

Smith and Taffler. December 1995. "The Incremental Effect of Narrative Accounting Information in Corporate Annual Reports." *Journal of Business Finance & Accounting* 22, no. 8, pp. 0306–686X.

Tysiac, K. July 2017. "How Family Businesses can Plan for the Future." *Journal of Accountancy* 224, no. 1, pp. 1–7.

Wakefield, J., and P. Thambar. August 2019. "Applying Target Costing to the Service Sector: Sunline Auto Insurance Case Issues In Accounting Education." *American Accounting Association* 34, no. 3, 1–19. doi: 10.2308/iace-52427

Ward, C.L., and S.K. Lowe. Winter 2017. "Cultural Impact of International financial Standards on the Comparability of Financial Statements." *International Journal of Business, Accounting, and Finance* 11, no 1, pp. 46–56.

White, M., I. Anistol, and M. Anistol. 2015. "Adoption of Activity Based Costing. Four Perspective Model as an Illustration." *Business Studies Journal* 10, pp. 66–83.

About the Authors

Roger Hussey is a fellow of the Association of Chartered Certified Accountants (FCCA) and received his MSc in industrial relations and his PhD in financial communications from the University of Bath. He worked in industry as an accountant for several years before moving to the Industrial Relations Unit at St Edmund Hall, Oxford University, as director of research into employee communications. Following a 6-year period at Oxford University, he accepted a position at the University of the West of England as Deloitte and Touche professor of financial reporting. Roger is professor emeritus at the University of the West of England and the University of Windsor, Canada.

Audra Ong is a professor of accounting at the University of Windsor, Canada. She received her PhD in accounting from the University of the West of England, her MBA from the University of Wales, Cardiff, and her BSc in accounting from Queen's University, Belfast (UK). Audra has published in both professional and academic journals and presented papers at numerous national and international conferences.

Index

OTHER TITLES IN THE FINANCIAL ACCOUNTING, AUDITING, AND TAXATION COLLECTION

Mark Bettner, Bucknell University, and Michael Coyne, Fairfield University, Editors

- *Sustainability Performance and Reporting* by Irene M. Herremans
- *Applications of Accounting Information Systems* by David M. Shapiro
- *Forensic Accounting and Financial Statement Fraud, Volume II* by Zabi Rezaee
- *A Non-Technical Guide to International Accounting* by Roger Hussey and Audra Ong
- *Forensic Accounting and Financial Statement Fraud, Volume I* by Zabihollah Rezaee
- *The Tax Aspects of Acquiring a Business, Second Edition* by Eugene W. Seago
- *The Story Underlying the Numbers* by Veena S. Iyer
- *Corporate Governance in the Aftermath of the Global Financial Crisis, Volume II* by Zabihollah Rezaee
- *Corporate Governance in the Aftermath of the Global Financial Crisis, Volume I* by Zabihollah Rezaee
- *Pick a Number, Second Edition* by Roger Hussey and Audra Ong
- *Using Accounting & Financial Information, Second Edition* by Mark S. Bettner
- *Accounting Fraud, Second Edition* by Gary Giroux
- *A Refresher in Financial Accounting* by Faisal Sheikh
- *Accounting History and the Rise of Civilization, Volume II* by Gary Giroux
- *Accounting History and the Rise of Civilization, Volume I* by Gary Giroux

Concise and Applied Business Books

The Collection listed above is one of 30 business subject collections that Business Expert Press has grown to make BEP a premiere publisher of print and digital books. Our concise and applied books are for...

- Professionals and Practitioners
- Faculty who adopt our books for courses
- Librarians who know that BEP's Digital Libraries are a unique way to offer students ebooks to download, not restricted with any digital rights management
- Executive Training Course Leaders
- Business Seminar Organizers

Business Expert Press books are for anyone who needs to dig deeper on business ideas, goals, and solutions to everyday problems. Whether one print book, one ebook, or buying a digital library of 110 ebooks, we remain the affordable and smart way to be business smart. For more information, please visit www.businessexpertpress.com, or contact sales@businessexpertpress.com.